SpringerWienNewYork

Anton Weber • Schahram Dustdar

Haptic Systems Architecture Modeling

SpringerWienNewYork

Dipl.Ing. Anton Weber
Julius Blum GmbH
Nelkenweg 2
6973 Höchst
Austria
antonhweber@googlemail.com

Dr. Schahram Dustdar
Vienna University of Technology
Distributed Systems Group (DSG)
Information Systems Institute
Argentinierstraße 8/184-1
1040 Vienna
Austria
dustdar@infosys.tuwien.ac.at

SpringerWienNewYork is a part of Springer Science+Business Media
springer.at

Printed on acid-free and chlorine-free bleached paper
SPIN: 80053203

With 97 Figures

Library of Congress Control Number: 2011939754

ISBN 978-3-7091-0754-6 e-ISBN 978-3-7091-0755-3
DOI 10.1007/978-3-7091-0755-3
SpringerWienNewYork

Preface

Haptic System Architecture Modeling introduces a new haptic approach to create system architectures. It can be used to develop, build, communicate, and file architectures. The idea is to build a system's architecture with the help of Lego. Each element in a system is represented by a composition of Lego bricks. The working team can create the system's architecture by combining every single representation to one big building. In order to guarantee further proceeding of the resulting architecture a tool is presented. With this tool the architects have the possibility to read in the building using RFID, to configure it using the provided functionalities, and to export it to ACME or CTB.

Contents

Chapter 1
Introduction

1.1 Motivation

The professions of software and system architecture are very young and fast evolving subjects of software development. Not long ago it has not been understood as an area of software engineering. Now numerous experts engage themselves in developing general valid definitions which provide a common understanding of what software architecture as a profession by its own actually is.

For now understanding software architecture as a building plan for, an overview on and a way of documentation for software, is sufficient. Experts have different opinions on how such an architecture should be developed, built, communicated, and conserved. Many techniques have been evolved to use them for dealing with software architecture such as UML-diagrams (Unified Modeling Language) or numerous architectural description languages (ADL). Working with such instruments often makes the assignment of an architect not open to teamwork. Drawing diagrams or building architectures in front of one computer per se is not very efficient to be done as a team. Even small barriers such as not enough space in front of the single working place can inhibit the possibility of teamwork.

Complex drawings using defined diagrams like UML or outputs of ADLs can often not be understood by non-experts such as the client who actually ordered the product. Explanatory discussions are needed to be held between the architects and the various stakeholders who do not share the understanding of the often sophisticated and abstract results created by the developers.

This book introduces a new approach of dealing with the development and communication of system architectures. It is meant to be settled right at the beginning of the process of software and system design. With it, architects can use a more intuitive and haptic approach. In that manner, in the process of architectural development, embedded engineers use pre-defined 3-dimensional building block compositions to construct a first prototype of their desired architecture.

A. Weber and S. Dustdar, *Haptic Systems Architecture Modeling*,
DOI 10.1007/978-3-7091-0755-3_1,

Such an approach could be dealt with in a more intuitive way for both the experts and the stakeholders. It provides the possibility of unrestricted teamwork. And because of its tangible, concrete condition it is a constructive way to communicate the architecture behind the composition to stakeholders who don't share the expertise of the architects.

1.2 Problem

To provide an approach which offers the handling of 3-dimensional compositions such constructions are defined in two ways. First the construction itself needs to be defined. That is, questions arise such as: which material should the composition be built of? What dimensions should the composition have? What kind of shape should the composition be of? Has the composition to be single-colored? What color should the composition have at all? Then the actual meaning behind the construction needs to be described and mapped to a real definition. That is, a specific composition has to represent a specific component in software architecture.

Beneath the problem of the real-world compositions arises the problem of how a software architecture built by real units can be processed by a computer so that a constructive proceeding of the architecture itself can be guaranteed.

This book proposes a realization of the above mentioned approach and introduces solutions to the problems which arise of such an approach.

1.3 Outline

Chapter 1 introduces the topic of the book, its motivation and the actual problem.

Chapter 2 examines state of the art definitions of software and system architecture and what approach architects follow nowadays to solve their assignment.

Chapter 3 presents the actual new approach, its details, and the gains resulting through it. It also provides various explanations for how the approach is realized.

Chapter 4 shows the documentation of the presented HSAM-Tool. It describes its graphical user interfaces as well as their background operations and data handling.

Chapter 5 maps the real-world compositions to their actual meanings. The architectural components are described and the real-world compositions are defined and illustrated.

Chapter 6 stages a case study. A fictitious system is build and realized using Haptic System Architecture Modeling.

Chapter 7 concludes the book, presents some possible improvements of the introduced system and shows possible enhancements.

The *Addendum* presents a user guide for the presented tool. It describes its main functions, its buildup, and provides numerous screenshots along with descriptions.

Chapter 2
Software Architecture Today

There is no all-explaining and globally valid definition for either software architecture or system architecture. Many experts have their own approach and way to define their field of action. But all of them have at least one thing in common: They all think experience is a key element for building software and/or system architectures.

In Sect. 2.1 some possible definitions of software architecture and the ideas behind them are pointed out. In Sect. 2.2 definitions of system architectures are defined and analyzed. After defining those two areas nowadays common approaches to find architectures for software and computer systems are shown in Sect. 2.3.

2.1 What is Software Architecture?

Shaw and David define software architecture the following way:

> Structural issues include the organization of a system as a composition of components; global control structures; the protocols for communication, synchronization, and data access; the assignment of functionality to design elements; the composition of design elements; physical distribution; scaling and performance, dimensions of evolution; end selection among design alternatives. This is the software architecture level of design.[1]

More abstract:

> The architecture of a software system defines that system in terms of computational components and interactions among those components.[2]

[1] Shaw and David 1996, p. 1.

[2] Shaw and David 1996, p. 3.

A. Weber and S. Dustdar, *Haptic Systems Architecture Modeling*,
DOI 10.1007/978-3-7091-0755-3_2, © Springer-Verlag/Wien 2012

In comparison to the definitions mentioned above Vogel has a more general approach to define architecture for software. In his view architectures of any kind always strongly include social and organizational emphases. So it is not only a pure technical discipline. Also an architecture cannot bear any details of the system or software itself. Its intention has to be building fundamental columns on which in a later process of constructing the software the details can be evolved. It has to provide a manageable view over the complexity of the problem.[3]

> Die Software-Architektur eines Systems beschreibt dessen Software-Struktur respektive dessen – Strukturen, dessen Software-Bausteine sowie deren sichtbaren Eigenschaften und Beziehungen zueinander.[4]

Another definition is provided by Bass:

> The software architecture of a program or computing system is the structure of structures of the system, which comprise software components, the externally visible properties of those components, and the relationships among them.[5]

Bass sees software architecture as a result of an ongoing cycle of technical, business and social influences. In turn software architecture also affects the corresponding environments. They call this during a design process existing situation the architecture business cycle (ABC). In this cycle Bass sees the architect and its product to be influenced by a variety of stakeholders, the technical environment and his own experience. Stakeholder would be customers, end users, the developing organization's management, marketing and the maintenance organization. Each of them has other priorities to what the architecture has to feature. For example the customer who has to pay for the product would like to be the costs as low as possible. He'd even accept a loss of usability to lower the costs. This in turn is the opposite of what the end user would like the product to be. He who actually uses the resulting program wants to work with a product which provides a high level of usability.[6]

2.2 What is System Architecture?

Vogel provides a definition for a system in a general aspect:

> Ein System ist eine Einheit, die aus miteinander interagierenden Software- und Hardware-Bausteinen besteht sowie zur Erfüllung eines fachlichen Ziels existiert. Es kommuniziert zur Erreichung seines Ziels mit seiner Umwelt und muss den durch die Umwelt vorgegebenen Rahmenbedingungen Rechnung tragen.[7]

---

[3] Cf. Vogel et al. 2005.

[4] Vogel et al. 2005, S. 46.

[5] Bass and et al. 1998.

[6] Cf. Bass et al. 1998, pp. 6–10.

[7] Vogel et al. 2005, S. 44.

Consequently for Vogel a system is more than just components of software. Software architecture is therefore just a part of the architecture of a whole system. However, they both are connected very tight and therefore affect each other. The system is embedded in an organizational environment with which it interacts.[8]

2.3 Today's Approach

In Vogel's[9] opinion architectural awareness is what makes an architect either successful or not. The architect has to decide a lot of decisions during the process of design. However, the fundamentals of those decisions are very dynamical. New demands and specification expressed by the stakeholders, arriving of new technology, or even new experiences of the architect himself can influence the making of decisions and so also the development of the architecture.

2.3.1 The Proceeding

Further on Vogel states in order to prevent any unpredictable events the architectural awareness should work like a letter case. With its help the architect can deposit experiences and acquired knowledge into mental boxes and also fetch them whenever he needs them. This letter case is spanning a regulation framework within which the architect creates and develops system architecture.

Within this regulation framework Vogel defines six main dimensions[10]:

- What – architectures and disciplines in architecture
- Where – perspectives on architecture
- Why – specifications for architecture
- Wherewith – instruments in architecture
- Who – organizations and individuals
- How – approach to architecture

Those dimensions provide the rough fundamentals for the letter case. They assure a meaningful breakup between each other so that they can be expanded independently and still they are extensive enough so that all different approaches to architecture can be conceptualized. With the help of such a regulation framework, in Vogel's opinion, the architect can attend to fundamental questions and therefore systematically orientate himself in practical cases.

[8] Vogel et al. 2005, S. 44–45.

[9] Cf. Vogel et al. 2005, S. 24–30.

[10] Cf. Vogel et al. 2005, S. 26–27.

The following section presents the fundamental dimensions of the regulation framework how Vogel defines them[11]:

- What

The architect should be capable of defining, describing and comparing architecture to other architectures even of different subjects and/or professions. Furthermore due to the high requirements of software architecture distinct disciplines of architecture established themselves. Vogel lists the following disciplines: software architecture, data architecture, architecture of integration, network architecture, security architecture, system management architecture, enterprise architecture. The architect often has to decide which kind of architecture he wants to realize.

- Where

Architectures of any kind are very complex and often unmanageable as one piece. Therefore the architect needs to reduce its complexity by only examine and handle manageable parts of the ensemble. To do so he works on so called architecture layers or levels always knowing what kind of connection the layer has to and how the layer fits to the rest of the architecture. On different layers the architect can use different instruments. He can even adopt different views to the layer. Views should lower the complexity for the architect and should make a systematically approach to the architecture possible.

- Why

Software architectures have numerous specifications to fulfill. Those specifications in turn can be classified by their kinds. For Vogel such classes are: Specifications by an organization, by a system, by a component, by the time of development, by the runtime and organizational conditions. An architect needs to be aware of the different kinds of specifications in order to design a goal-oriented IT-system.

- Wherewith

Every architect gets to know a huge variety of instruments which can be used to create architecture during his professional life. He keeps a classification system for all these instruments regarding their relevance to the architect in mind. Such instruments can range from conceptual principles to concrete technologies. Principles are approved instruments of architectural design. Fundamental concepts use such principles to enable the architect to use them in his architecture. Architectural styles and patterns, again, rely on such concepts and principles. Styles and patterns are successful and approved solutions for a thriving architecture. Patterns often also are used to document the structure of architecture. When a specific solution for an architecture was outstanding the architect can use the whole

[11] Cf. Vogel et al. 2005, S. 30–38.

structure of it as a reference to which he can rely in the future. Because it is important to not only create architecture but also vulgarize it to all involved stakeholders, developers and other individuals the architect also needs a collection of documentary instruments. Moreover, the practice of creating architecture for software and IT-systems generated specific architectural structures which provide basic technologies to build such approved structures. And last but not least the architect needs to be aware of updates of such instruments to in turn update his collection so that he can provide the most proven solution for his clients.

- Who

As Vogel mentioned before an architect needs to vulgarize all the working steps, the proceeding and the architecture itself to an amount of individuals. In order to do so most effectually and successfully he needs to possess expertise in social contact.

- How

The goal of an architectural design is to provide a fundamental structure onto which a system can be build. The architect can access a collection of instruments, interchange information with others and take different views on to his work in order to reach the optimal architecture to fulfill all the requirements and specifications. In Vogel's opinion, for an architect to distinguish himself as a successful architect he needs to be capable of working systematically. So he needs to work iteratively through the procedure model provided by Vogel: creating a business case, understanding the specifications, designing the architecture, vulgarizing the architecture, implementing the architecture.

The whole process of development is done through an iterative-incremental process. In those iterations the architect's tasks consist of a combination of above mentioned five actions. Whereas in the beginning of the process the tasks envelop rather the actions of creating a business case and understanding the specification and in the further preceding of the process the tasks consist of communicating the architecture and implementing it.[12]

The following will show the architect's role during the elaboration of the main actions[13]:

- Creating a business case: During this action the characterization of the task and the goal takes place. The architect has the role of a technical adviser to ensure the technical feasibility.
- Understanding the specifications: The architect finds and analyzes the specification and tries to solve inconsistent requirements.
- Designing the architecture: This is the actual task where the architect designs the architecture. To do so he has a variety of instruments as mentioned above. Subsequent those instruments get described more detailed.

[12] Cf. Vogel et al. 2005, S. 274.

[13] Cf. Vogel et al. 2005, S. 275.

– Vulgarizing the architecture: It is of great interest to the architect that all the stakeholders have a good understanding of the architecture. It influences their further work and ability of success. So in this task the architect makes sure that all stakeholders understand the architecture.
– Implementing the architecture: In order to make sure the implementation of the system is conforming to the architecture the architect verifies this during this task.

So far the today's approach was roughly outlined. In the next step the architect's instruments get described more detailed.

It was mentioned above that an architect makes use of a variety of instruments. With the help of such resources he designs, concepts, communicates and documents his architectures. Those are[14]:

– Architectural principles: There are a big number of architectural principles, such as modularity, information hiding, abstraction, separation of concerns, etc., which have proven themselves to be useful and constructive. It doesn't depend on the use of such principles whether the out coming architecture is a good or a bad one. But the lack of fundamental principles within an architecture is a strong sign that it can be a weak model of a specific architecture. There are possibilities that one principle is conflicting with another and thus the two can't be combined in a single architecture but this should always be deliberate and the consciously omitting of an appropriate principle should always be well documented.
– Architectural concepts: There are fundamental concepts for how to build an architecture which the architect can access. Those are widely used and highly approved. Such concepts would be procedural approaches, object orientation, component orientation, etc.
– Architectural styles: A less abstract instrument for the architect would be architectural styles. Such styles developed from the experience that they have already repeatedly been useful to solve a specific problem in an architecture. They are solutions to recurrent occurring and well known problems. The architectural style of a system describes the founding structure of the system itself and allows categorizing it and comparing it to other systems. Such styles[15] would be pipes and filters, hierarchical layers, rule-based systems, event systems, etc.
– Architectural patterns: Patterns are like styles a more concrete support for the architect. They again are a solution possibility for a series of specific problems. Moreover, patterns provide a concrete method of resolution to solve a precise problem. Such patterns are proxies, broker, etc.
– Architecture as reference: When an architect uses a whole architecture as a reference he has got a complete solution for a certain problem area. Such a solution combines general architectural knowledge and expertise with specific requirements. The architect can use such a reference whenever he encounters an architectural problem which has been solved similar before.

[14] Cf. Vogel et al. 2005, S. 112–194.

[15] Cf. Shaw and David 1996, p. 20.

2.3.2 *Instruments for Documentation*

So far actions that are taken by the architects have been listed. However, it is not the only problem for them to actually create an architecture but also to write it down and document it. The right choice of instrument to document the built architecture is very important to communicate it to all the stakeholders. It is a great influence to how easy the various stakeholders can understand the architecture. Different instruments can provide a different sort of view onto the architecture which in turn can be more practical in communicating the architecture to a specific stakeholder. That is the end user who actually has to work with the system at the end has a different approach to the whole system than a programmer who will implement the system. Different views provide different types of information about the architecture. So the architecture needs to be presented to each stakeholder as clear and as understandable as possible in order to let them be as most constructive as possible. To do so the architects have a variety of documentation instruments. The following will shortly present the instruments UML (Unified Modeling Language), ADL (Architecture Description Language), DSL (Domain Specific Language) and Acme (an ADL) (Fig. 2.1).

- UML[16]: The Unified Modeling Language is the result of the merging of a lot of sublanguages. In its evolution it combines and adapts more and more other languages to result as a single valid one. Today UML is available as version 2.1.1[17] and still evolving. The positive part about UML is that it provides a lot of different views onto one architecture at the same time. But because it is a relative young standard it does not include all kinds of components so that an architect may use another element to substitute the missing one. To provide those views UML comes with a variety of different diagrams. Vogel contrasts the different view onto an architecture with the accordingly UML diagrams.[18]
- ADL[19]: In Architecture Description Languages a component features a very central role. ADLs approve the precise design of architectures before they are implemented. That makes it possible for the architect to determine whether the architecture has any errors or problems and whether it complies with the requirements which should from it. Moreover, the attributes of the architecture can be analyzed. So an ADL has a good qualification to design, analyze and simulate an architecture before its implementation as a system. Additionally they feature the following[20]:

[16] Cf. Vogel et al. 2005, S. 197.

[17] OMG – Object Management Group.

[18] Vogel et al. 2005, S. 199–200.

[19] Cf. Vogel et al. 2005, S. 201.

[20] Vogel et al. 2005, S. 202.

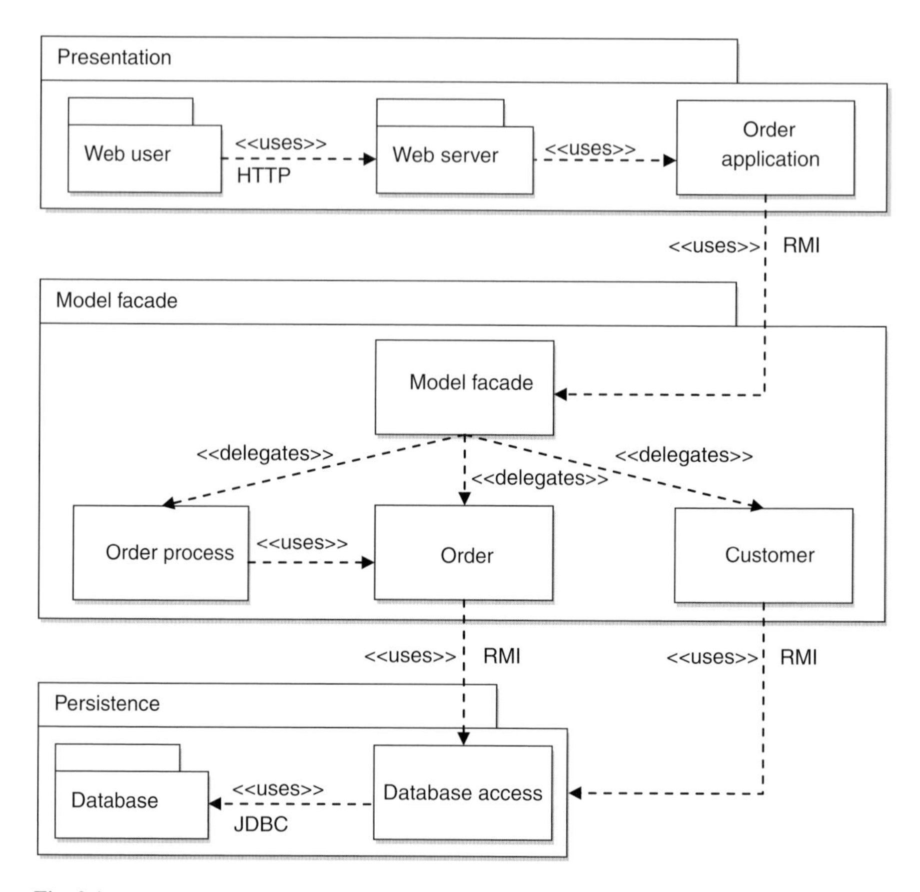

Fig. 2.1 An example for an UML-diagram (Cf. Vogel et al. 2005, S. 201)

- Formal representation of architecture using textual and graphic notations at a very high level of abstraction
- Readability for human and machine
- Possibility for analysis various architectural aspects like completeness, consistency, performance, etc.
- Partly featuring of automated code generation

As mentioned before ADLs concentrate in building an architecture out of components. For those components it describes its data and data integrity as well as their interfaces of any kind. In order to let the components interact among each other ADLs inaugurate connectors. They connect components to each other and determine the rules under which the components can interact. Last but not least ADLs define a architectural configuration which defines the architectural structure by determining which components are connected through which connectors (Fig. 2.2).[21]

[21] Vogel et al. 2005, S. 204.

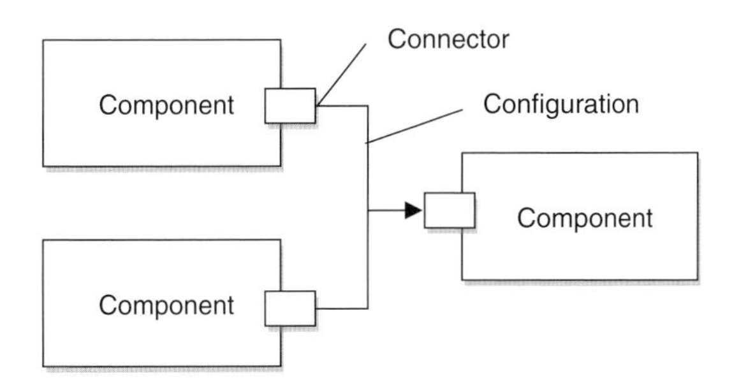

Fig. 2.2 ADL core concept (Cf. Vogel et al. 2005, S. 206)

- DSL[22]: DSLs are description languages specific for according domains. The concepts behind it are well formed for the appropriate problem and therefore advantageous over normal ADLs.
- Acme[23]: It was developed out of the need to provide interoperability between varieties of other instruments for architectural design. Acme provides three essential capabilities:
  - Architectural interchange: Architects who don't use Acme are capacitated to use their ADL with Acme so that they have a greater choice of what design tools they want to use in order to analyze their architecture. On the other side Acme users can incorporate with other ADLs.
  - Extensible foundation for new architecture design and analysis tools: Because of its fundamental and common approach to architectural design Acme can be used as basis for other more specialized languages still providing the interchangeability. This is reducing costs and time for development of the new language.
  - Architecture description: Actually developed as an interchange tool it evolved as a standalone description language including architectural styles, types, structures plus properties for all elements with which easily software architectures can be created.

2.3.3 Weak Points

Nonetheless above mentioned architect's instruments do have their weak points. As Vogel[24] states in a list of handicaps of ADLs their first weak point is that it is not yet clarified which aspects of system architecture an ADL should even cover. There is no distinct determination of what needs to be documented by an ADL. This is so far going that it is not even specified what ADL should be called on what problem. So if

---

[22] Cf. Vogel et al. 2005, S. 206.

[23] ABLE – Architecture Based Languages and Environments 2007.

[24] Vogel et al. 2005, S. 202.

an architect needs to document a system architecture of a specific domain he still is spoilt for choice of what kind of ADL he should even use.

That is because there is no single ADL which excels itself as the one standard ADL. They are all specialized to be used for specific domains. And still there is no single ADL for each domain. Each of it is strongly specialized in its own way. Because of their specialization there is no uniform structure amongst the ADLs. Each structure is adapted to their need in the particular domain. The more sophisticated structure supports an ADL's ability to analyze and simulate an architecture of a specific domain.

Hence, a problem of more practical origin arises. Notations of the ADLs also vary due to different structures. But what makes them alike is that their notations are more or less difficult to process and until now there is no support for them by commercial tools.

Another more practical difference between ADLs is the targeted user of an ADL. Some of them support a direct code framework conversion of the created architecture. Those kinds of ADL address architects who are more into the actual implementation of their system whereas other ADLs which do not support such a conversion offer more freedom in the choice of how an architect wishes the architecture to be implemented. It is more of a problem to the actual programmer. ADLs of the second kind keep code away from the architecture and thus make the project more modular.

Moreover, ADLs are still a matter of research. They are often developed by research projects at universities and therefore not really established as a tool for commercial use due to constant development and alteration.

Although ADLs still undergo ambitious and concrete development there is no clear delimitation to other kinds of instruments. For example they still use a broad spectrum of UML-diagrams in order to illustrate the architecture. Whereas it is of interest to use existing technology it is still a problem of independence. So ADLs which rely too much on other instruments are more dependent than ADLs which try to realize the whole architecture with their own methods. On the other hand ADLs which support known technology can be more understandable and more open to others for further development of architectures and development of the ADL itself.

Over all in Vogel's opinion it can be said that ADLs are less general than other instruments. This as a result does not award them with a qualification for the use to describe general aspects of architecture. They can simply not be used for that matter. So ADLs are more and more developed for the needs of a specific domain and therefore become more and more specialized for their area of interest which on the other side deprives them as a candidate to describe more general architectural aspects.

In contrast to ADLs UML as the de-facto standard is more concentrated on classes and objects. Whereas for ADLs components and the connectors between the components are in focus of processing for UML it is more the composition of classes and objects. ADLs do have a more precise syntax adapted for the domain the ADL is in use. They focus on interfaces of the components and the connectors as a central concept. In comparison UML is not specialized in any way.

This enables a user to operate with it in a greater variety for documentation. But this causes the constricted possibilities to analyze and simulate the problem for which it was pulled up. Moreover, it can lead to a misunderstanding by stakeholders due to unclear semantics of notation. To partially avoid this problem UML can be extended with concepts of any kind (like ADL-concepts). This makes it more precise and accurate to a specific problem but again withdraws general aspects of UML.

Chapter 3
Introducing a New Approach

In this chapter a new approach called Haptic System Architecture Modeling (HSAM) for developing system architectures is presented. It is intended to support the architect in designing, creating, communicating, and documenting system architecture.

3.1 Overview

The innovative aspects for designing and handling system architectures with the help of HSAM derive from its intuitive and haptic ways of approaching architectural problems.

This is because the main idea of HSAM is to create a desired architecture of a system by using Lego[1] bricks. Hence the designing process becomes literally a modeling one. The architect does not operate with any diagrams, tables, or likewise instruments. Instead he creates representations of the system elements he wants to include in his project and combines them to form a construction which illustrates his system architecture.

Physical bricks surely require some sort of further handling to provide some sort of more sophisticated treatment of the architectures. For that a tool called the HSAM-Tool will be introduced. It provides functionalities to translate the physical building into a machine-readable format. With this tool the architect can read in the project using radio frequency technology, configure the system architecture by assigning properties to each element, and alter their default attributes; and in order to provide further processing of the building, he can export it to some more commonly used formats.

[1] LEGO Group 2007.

A. Weber and S. Dustdar, *Haptic Systems Architecture Modeling*,
DOI 10.1007/978-3-7091-0755-3_3,

The chain to build an architecture using HSAM can be split into the following tasks:

- Decide what elements are needed
- Integrate RFID transponders to elements
- Vary assembly of elements of same kind
- Build architecture
- Verify correctness of system
- Read in the architecture to the HSAM-Tool
- Configure information for each element
- Save project
- Export project

However, the sequence of the tasks is not mandatory as the whole process is an iterative procedure which necessitates the architect to consider and evaluate the outcomes of each step. Figure 3.1 shows an illustration of the workflow of HSAM and the connectivity of the tasks to each other. Still the tasks can be split into two domains which are:

- building an architecture (first five tasks of above shown list) and
- handling an architecture (last four tasks of above shown list)

3.2 Used Technology

The kind of approach HSAM follows requires special technology of both uncommon and more common use.

Frequent technology in this case would be radio frequency identification (RFID). It includes numerous standards which are used to be implemented in the domains of security and authentication, safety, convenience, and process efficiency.[2]

For software aspects rather uncommon technology would be the use of Lego bricks. Those are normally used as some kind of toy by children who can stack them to versatile buildings.

3.2.1 Lego

The LEGO group was founded 75 years ago with its head office located in Billund, Denmark. It is a traditional family business and is still headed by a descendant of the founder. As its vision it declares "*to inspire children to explore and challenge their own creative potential*".[3]

[2] Bhuptani and Moradpour 2005.

[3] LEGO Group 2007.

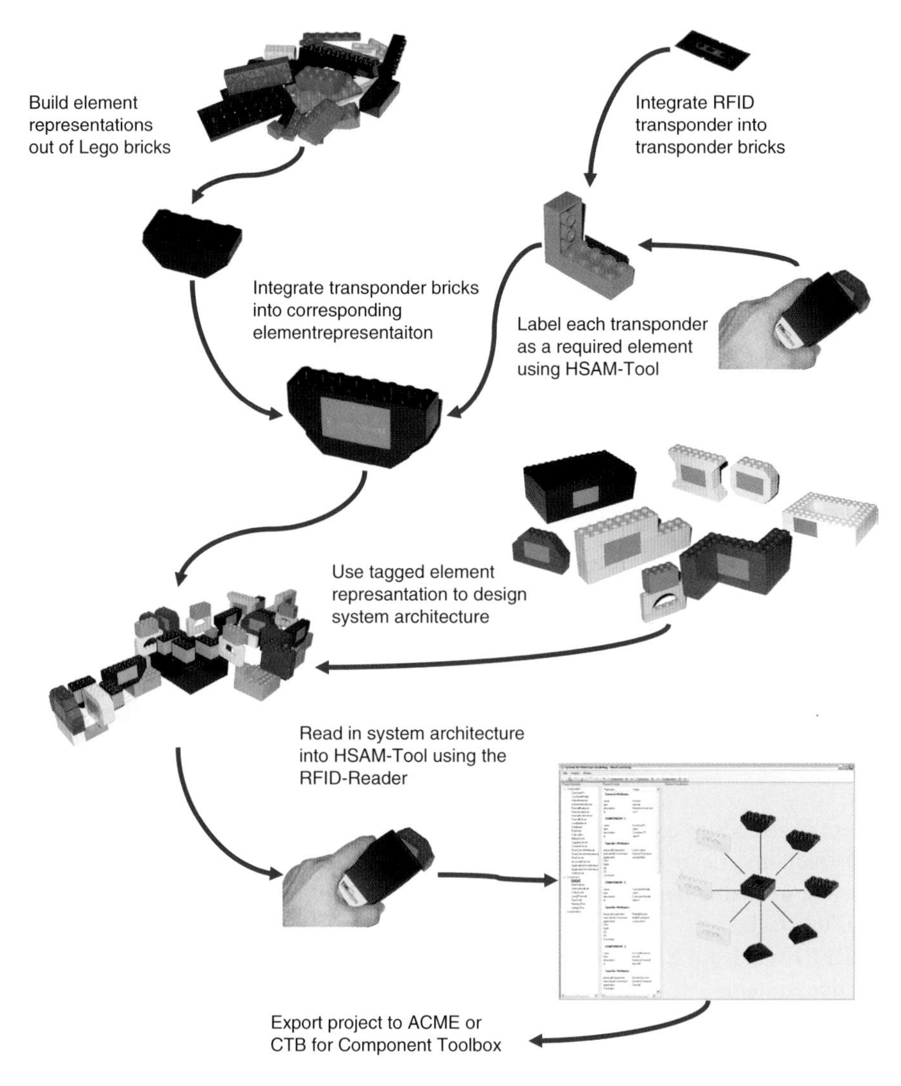
Build element
representations
out of Lego bricks
Integrate RFID
transponder into
transponder bricks
Integrate transponder bricks
into corresponding
elementrepresentaiton
Label each transponder
as a required element
using HSAM-Tool
Use tagged element
represantation to design
system architecture
Read in system architecture
into HSAM-Tool using the
RFID-Reader
Export project to ACME or
CTB for Component Toolbox

Fig. 3.1 Workflow of HSAM

For this book the most important product of the LEGO group is their Lego-brick:

> The brick in its present form was launched in 1958. The interlocking principle with its tubes makes it unique, and offers unlimited building possibilities.[4]

Using those bricks with their numerous differing appearances gives the architect the great potential to uniquely define a broad variety of elements. As listed in

[4] LEGO Group 2007.

Chap. 5 the bricks are used to standardize and define the look and feel of system architecture elements. Because of the unlimited alternatives of stacking the bricks onto each other a broad range of elements can be covered.

This also allows the creation of groupings which contain related system architecture elements. Such groups in each case enfold elements which are related in some kind in order to unite them by building them in either similar or contrary shape. For example a client and a server have a similar shape but are still built distinctly enough to notice their mannerism. The same is valid for publisher and subscriber which feature contrary shapes. To elements which are not from the same group they clearly differ in shape, size, and color so that it is obvious that they are not familiar.

Other reasons why Lego bricks were preferred over other sectional technologies are that they provide a broad variety of brick shapes and colors and the fact that it is so simple to combine and rearrange them. The contingent of different bricks by its own allows a nearly unlimited number for definitions of system architecture elements. Then the different kinds of colors again multiply this amount of possibilities. At last its simplicity lets the user work very efficiently, freely, and rapidly.

Section 5.2 will introduce how Lego bricks are used to represent system architecture elements.

3.2.2 RFID

There is a need for a technology which enables the further processing of the Lego constructions. Lego by itself features no possibilities to transfer its buildings to machine-readable languages. So RFID is the choice of what technology is used to bear this task.

RFID stands for Radio Frequency Identification and names an automated identification system.

> In a typical RFID system [...] objects are tagged with tiny radio transponders that carry certain data about the objects. The transponders (tags) transmit this data, through radio waves, to nearby readers, which collect and process the data accordingly.[5]

Because of its general applicability, RFID experiences a fast development and deployment in all kinds of domains. The most common areas of application are[6]:

- Security and authentication,
- Safety,
- Convenience, and
- Process efficiency.

---

[5] Bhuptani and Moradpour 2005, p. 4.

[6] Bhuptani and Moradpour 2005.

Security and authentication was one of the first domains to use RFID technology. It provides very simple possibilities to uniquely identify objects, persons, and/or animals. For safety aspects RFID systems are often used to create safer environments for employees and customers by sensing and monitoring the areas the users move in. RFID-enabled services can provide greater conveniences by loosening the bond between the system and the user. This often comes hand in hand with a more efficient process. Clearly, the industry is interested in improving their processes. Manufacturers often use RFID systems to monitor, track, and trace objects in order to enhance their business processes.

Bhuptani[7] outlines the history of RFID as follows and sees an auspicious future for the technology:

> As with radio, television, the transistor, and the computer, RFID saw only modest use for the first 30 years after its inception. Then, after an extended incubation period, a groundswell occurred, which culminated in the full-blown commercialization of RFID and a corresponding change to the lives of millions of people around the globe. RFID is now at the precipice of another major evolution that will change and improve the lives of businesses and individuals everywhere.

A basic RFID system consists of a tag (transponder), a reader (interrogator), and antennae (coupling devices) which need to be located at both sides of the system. Typically, the reader is connected to a computer which again is mostly part of a larger network of computers. The main feature of RFID systems is the contactless exchange of information. This is done by connecting (coupling) the tag and the reader through their antennae. There are a lot of different standards for the coupling operation. It can be accomplished either in an electromagnetic (backscatter) or in a magnetic (inductive) way. Both of the methods have their advantages and disadvantages which need to be balanced accordingly to the use of the system, the allowed costs, its size, speed, reading range, and accuracy. Another selection criterion is the frequency in which the RFID system is intended to be operating. The frequency affects speed and accuracy and is often chosen based on environmental conditions and/or standards and regulations.[8]

The RFID system used for this book features the following specifications:

- *Reader-model*: TAGmobi USB – Mifare[9]
- *Tag-model*: Smart Control Label – Mifare 1k[10]
- *Radiofrequency*: 13.56 MHz
- *Communication standard*: ISO 14443 A Mifare
- *Range*: up to 100 mm (short range RFID)

---

[7] Bhuptani and Moradpour 2005, p. 32.

[8] Cf. Bhuptani and Moradpour 2005.

[9] TAGnology RFID 2006a.

[10] TAGnology RFID 2006b.

The reader is connected to a computer via USB (universal serial bus) and through its driver addressed like a standard serial port. It operates at the Mifare standard at a frequency of 13.56 MHz. The transponders only support Mifare 1k ISO 14443.

Mifare is a trademark of NXP Semiconductors. Mifare 1k was first introduced in the year 1994 as a standard for contactless communication technology. Already 2 years later, it was used for its first deployment at a major transport project where it replaced the old ticketing system. Mifare 1k ISO 14443 A as used in this book features the following attributes[11]:

- Contactless transmission of data and supply energy (no battery needed)
- Operating distance: Up to 100 mm (depending on antenna geometry)
- Operating frequency: 13.56 MHz
- Fast data transfer: 106 kbit/s
- High data integrity: 16 bit CRC, parity bit coding, bit counting
- True anti-collision
- Typical ticketing transaction: <100 ms (including backup management)

The anti-collision algorithm would provide the feature to work with more than one tag in the field of operation at the same time. It assures that each tag is selected separately and that the data transaction is executed correctly. But in the case of this book, there will only be one single transponder in range for the reader to operate with due to the following two reasons. The first reason is the size of the transponders which is chosen very small to make them fit inside of a Lego brick but which also affects the range dramatically. As second reason is to mention that the Lego constructions used to represent a system's element require a certain size which means that there will not be room for two or more such compositions within the range of operation of the reader.

The reason why to use RFID as associational technology between Lego bricks and software is that it appeared to be the simplest and most efficient approach to be implemented. The tags can be easily attached inside of the bricks not affecting their ability to be stacked. The coupling overbears the thin plastic walls so that the exchange of information is guaranteed. On the other side of the RFID system the reader can be attached and installed to a computer. Also there are numerous libraries for using the reader in a program so that one does not have to do the implementation of all the functionalities concerning the reader over again.

Moreover, RFID won't constrict the freedom of buildings using Lego bricks. As Lego bricks were chosen because of their variety of building possibilities, the technology which provides further processing should not withdraw this feature. For example a graphical recognition system would have made problems finding elements which are hidden behind other elements. Using RFID this problem will not occur.

[11] NXP 2007.

Section 3.3.1.2 will introduce how the RFID transponders are integrated into the Lego representations of system architecture elements.

3.3 Walkthrough

This chapter deals with a detailed description on how to create a system architecture using Lego bricks and how to handle the building process using our program called the HSAM-Tool. It is split into two subsections. The first outlines the tasks of HSAM which mainly deal with Lego. It represents the instructions for how to actually build an architecture using Lego bricks. The second part shows how further processing of the Lego construction is provided. It introduces the HSAM-Tool and illustrates its main functionalities.

For instructions on how to access the introduced functionalities see Sect. 4.4.

3.3.1 Building an Architecture

The following will introduce the tasks of HSAM which mainly operate with Lego bricks. Only the task *Tag Elements* (Sect. 3.3.1.5) will make use of the HSAM-Tool. The sequence of how the tasks are listed does not imply the sequence of their execution. Of course all the other tasks need to be completed before the actual architecture can be built but the tasks before *Build Architecture* can be done in any order.

3.3.1.1 Define Elements

Defining the elements needed to design a system's architecture is the task to begin with. Of course it occurs that an architect needs to add additional elements to the system during the designing process, but he still wants to define some fundamental elements to build the architecture's main structure.

The architect then either selects the representation of each element out of a pool which holds prebuilt Lego compositions, or assembles each representation from a pool of loose Lego bricks based on the catalogue presented in Sect. 5.2.

3.3.1.2 Integrate RFID

In order to offer a machine readable approach, RFID transponders need to be integrated into certain Lego bricks which then are staked to each element in the task *Integrate Transponder-Bricks* (Sect. 3.3.1.3).

Those defined bricks are orange 2×4 bricks. Two of them attached on top of each other are needed to house one transponder.

Refer to Sect. 5.1.3.1 for instructions on how to integrate the chips into the Lego bricks.

3.3.1.3 Integrate Transponder-Bricks

This task is the second task to provide a machine readable approach. The special transponder equipped bricks need to be integrated into each element representation.

Depending on the size of a composition, it can be easy to assimilate the orange bricks. Generally, the transponder-bricks should be placed within the element in a way that it is obvious that the orange bricks tag the element.

The simplest way to do so is to fully surround the transponder-bricks with the bricks used to represent the element still assuring the access to the transponder for the RFID-reader. If this is not possible and the only way to attach the bricks is to stick them onto the element somewhere at the outside, then a spot where no other representation interferes the association should be chosen.

Refer to Sect. 5.1.3.2 for more directives on how to integrate the transponder-bricks.

3.3.1.4 Vary Shapes

Varying the shapes and sizes of elements of the same kind can be very useful. It enables the architect to immediately differentiate elements among each other and spot specific elements. He can assign special information to them like importance or attributes specific for the kind of element. Moreover, such variations are very handy for stakeholders who do not possess the backgrounds of a system architect because it makes it easier for them to understand the meaning of certain coherencies.

Such assignments should be documented separately and handed together with the finished end product so that following verifications and analyses of the architecture can work with the same information.

3.3.1.5 Tag Elements

Each transponder integrated into an element's representation needs to be referenced to the kind of element which houses its transponder-bricks in order to later correctly read in the architecture. This is done by using the HSAM-Tool.

First the user needs to make sure that a RFID-reader is connected to the computer and opened for use through the tool (see Sect. 4.4.11). When the prerequisites are fulfilled the user opens the *Refer Tag IDs*-Dialogue.

For each type of element the architect now chooses the right name in the upper *combobox* where it says "*< Choose Element >*". Then each element representation corresponding to the chosen element name is placed right in front of the reader so that coupling between reader and transponder is possible (refer to Sect. 3.3.2.1). For each element the architect hits the button *"Tag"* to issue the command to associate the transponder in range to the chosen element type.

For additional information on background operations of the dialogue see Sect. 4.4.12.

3.3.1.6 Build Architecture

Building an architecture doesn't require the transponders to be referred to their elements; but if they are not, the later read in will be complicated. This is because when the elements are combined to describe an architecture it might not be as easy and effective to tag them anymore because they are attached in a quirky way and hard for the reader to reach. This problem already occurs for the task *Read in the Architecture* (Sect. 3.3.2.1) so it should be avoided to be handled twice.

But just this problem has to be kept in mind when accomplishing this task and the task *Integrate Transponder-Bricks* (Sect. 3.3.1.3). It is important to situate the transponder-brick within the elements in a reachable way for the reader. The same is valid for the situation within the building of an architecture. The reader needs to be able to reach the transponders in order to successfully read in the project.

However, generally the architect uses already associated elements to create a system's architecture. To do so, elements need to be attached onto each other, whereas components always need to be connected to connectors. It will not be possible to directly link a component to another component (see Sect. 5.2 for allocation of elements into components and connectors) due to the read in process.

The attachment of elements to each other should always be chosen in a way that it is clear that the elements are connected. This is easily accomplished when the element representations are built big enough.

Due to the mere infinity of possibilities to attach the element representations to each other, there are innumerable ways to construct a system. Although this may be cause for discussion to the architect, it also offers free thinking about the possibilities of how the system can be compiled.

See Chap. 6 for an example of a built architecture.

3.3.1.7 Verify Architecture

The last task and controlling task for building an architecture is to verify and validate the built construction by comparing it to the real system. If the building represents a system which is about to be realized then it should be validated by comparing it to the requirements it should fulfill.

It is more effective is to continuously verify the architecture during the actual building process. This obviates errors which could pervade the whole system and thus improve the system and the designing process as a whole.

3.3.2 *Handle the Construction*

The following will list tasks that introduce various functionalities of the HSAM-Tool. In order to guarantee further processing of the built Lego construction only the tasks *Read in the Architecture* and *Export the Architecture* need to be accomplished.

3.3.2.1 Read in the Architecture

In order to correctly read in an architecture, each transponder integrated into an element's representation needs to be referenced to the kind of element which houses its transponder-bricks (see Sect. 3.3.1.5).

Before using RFID functionalities of the HSAM-Tool, a reader needs to be connected (see Sect. 4.4.11). When both prerequisites are fulfilled, a correct read in is possible and the user opens the *Read in Elements*-Dialogue.

Generally, when using the reader at a transponder which is embedded in transponder-bricks, the reader should be placed with its front end very close to the side of the bricks where the transponder is situated. Otherwise coupling will not be possible due to the shorter range of the small tags (see Fig. 3.2).

The read in of an architecture requires the architect to always first read in a connecting element and then the components connected through that element. This is because of the HSAM-Tool which otherwise could not establish the connection between the components. If accidently a component of one connector was left out while another connector was selected, simply reselect the first connector to assign the missed component to it. The connector will not be created twice.

So after reading in a connector, read in its connecting components and move on to the next connector and its components until all elements of the architecture are handled.

The data structure of the read in architecture is in the style of the ACME-ADL. This means that the main entities are components and connectors. As a component holds ports as sub-entities a connector holds roles. Each of those entities and sub-entities additionally can hold various properties and default attributes such as name, type, etc.

Fig. 3.2 Possible coupling

The actual connection between a connector and a component is recorded as a value of an attribute of a role. This value represents the reference to a component's port so that all components can be reached through the connector which holds the appropriate roles.

Refer to Sect. 4.2 for additional information on the inner data management.

3.3.2.2 Configure the Architecture

The HSAM-Tool provides functionalities to configure the read in architecture. Configuration means that it is possible to add, delete, and edit properties of each data entity and to edit their default properties. Moreover, properties for the whole project can be defined, edited, and deleted.

Configuring the elements of an architecture enables the architect to enrich the construction with additional information. This in turn allows the architect to differentiate between elements of the same kind which are equipped with only default values for their attributes and default properties. Moreover, the information adapted through the HSAM-Tool will later be critical information for the exportation process which takes advantage of the attributes and properties to generate a particularly meaningful output file.

As shown in Sect. 4.4, all elements and their sub-entities are listed somehow in either a list or a tree. To access the corresponding configuration window simply double-click on the element.

Refer to the appropriate subsection of Sect. 4.4 for additional information on the user interfaces.

3.3.2.3 Store the Architecture

This and the following task are not essential anymore for the actual designing process. The HSAM-Tool provides storing functionalities. A project can either be saved as a XML-file, as a composition which can be added to later projects, or both.

For information on a saved project refer to Sect. 4.2 and for the composition savings refer to Sects. 4.4.2 and 4.4.10.

3.3.2.4 Export the Architecture

To offer further processing of the outcomes of Haptic System Architecture Modeling the HSAM-Tool provides functionalities to export a project to the ADL ACME or as a CTB-file which is used by the Component Toolbox introduced by Hofstetter.[12]

---

[12] Hofstetter 2007.

3.4 Discussion

This chapter deals with the advantages and disadvantages of the Haptic System Architecture Modeling approach. First, the advantages are listed and fortified. Then some disadvantages are shown and improvements suggested.

3.4.1 Advantages

The first advantage Haptic System Architecture Modeling reveals is its intuitivism. Once the user gets clear about the implied meanings of each element, he will have no further problems to easily construct a system's architecture. To know if the result is valid demands indeed some background knowledge of the system the user wants to create but still the user is capable of building it. There is no learning of complicated syntax needed. This makes the approach accessible for everyone.

Due to its straightforwardness the approach is excellent applicable to communicate and present an architecture to its various stakeholders. Even to such stakeholders who are not in possession of the knowledge a system architect usually has. All a viewer needs is a mapping of each Lego composition to its meaning in the real world. No further information is needed to understand the underlying structure of an architecture. Additional descriptive information is provided by the HSAM-Tool with which each element can be investigated.

As the whole structure of a complex architecture can be seen and captured at just one glance, it is easier for stakeholders who were not included in the building process to understand its assembly and the meanings resulting from it. This is because the Lego construction provides an excellent overview on the project.

On account of its haptic nature, Haptic System Architecture Modeling supports teamwork. All architects involved in the building process can build the system together at the same time. This boosts the exchange of information between the architects at an early stage of development. This in turn eliminates misunderstandings before they possibly arise. They can even learn from each other while they are in action and provide feedback while the building process still persists.

Due to the design of the HSAM-Tool, it is very simple to extend Haptic System Architecture Modeling with additional elements, information on elements, and their mappings. In order to do so, there is a definition of the Lego composition of the element required. To integrate it into the tool the configuration xml-file needs to be adapted. The new element has to be defined in the same structure as the already existing ones have. There is no additional task to do to successfully integrate a new element.

As mentioned before, Hofstetter[13] introduces a tool called Component Toolbox. As HSAM-Tool provides a function to export a system architecture to the format

[13] Hofstetter 2007.

required by Component Toolbox, the possibility of further processing of the architecture is guaranteed. With this tool the architect has an instrument to create a software architecture which is based on the system architecture provided by HSAM. So there is no overhead of documentation needed, no numerous diagrams. It gets easier for the architects to communicate the actual outcome because they don't need to spend resources to define what the product should be based on.

3.4.2 Disadvantages

Unfortunately, the use of Lego bricks can also be seen as a barrier. The element representations are not self-explanatory. There is still mapping information required which uniquely assigns a representation to its meaning. However, the compositions could be built in a way so that the actual element can be deduced by its shape and looks. Also consuetude and constant practice help to keep the meanings of the representations in mind.

Building an architecture using HSAM demands from the architects to follow the recommendations of the representations catalogue presented in Sect. 5.2. Representations can easily lose their shapes because of inaccurate building habits. There is no possibility to constrict the constructions due to the fact that Lego bricks can be attached to each other in multiple ways. This is because the architect needs to work consistently.

Of course the catalogue of element representations is by far not completed. Several elements of various domains could be added and defined, as well as domains per se based on the model of families in ACME could be established. Besides, the shape of each representation needs to be validated precisely. Due to the fact that not all elements are part of the case study in Chap. 6 the shapes of the unused ones did not need to prove themselves.

The HSAM-Tool is a prototype and by far not well enough implemented to claim perfect operation. Of course this could be improved. Additional features could be provided like a better visualization of an architecture. Maybe the chain of actions can be enhanced. Also a diversity of exportation formats could be realized to gain more possibilities to work with HSAM.

Chapter 4
Implementation

This chapter introduces the details on the implementation of the HSAM-Tool. First, a class diagram is presented. After that, the most important classes will be handled to explain special behaviors. Then the internal data management of the tool will be explicated. In the following part, the interface to further programs is shown in form of the exporting formats. And at last the graphical user interfaces are pictured and explained and their most important underlying operations are identified.

The HSAM-Tool is as important for the modeling process as the Lego bricks. It provides the functionalities to read in the architecture, to represent the architecture, to configure its elements, and to export the architecture to other languages like ACME and CTB-XML, as well as the creation of a whole project without using the RFID functionalities.

4.1 Class Diagram

The class diagram shown in Fig. 4.1 illustrates all classes used in the HSAM-Tool but only lists their most important functions and properties. For a detailed listing see the Addendum for instructions on how to reach the detailed documentation.

In the following, the classes and their most important functions are explained in more detail.

4.1.1 Class: Program

The class *Program* provides the main entry point for the HSAM-Tool by featuring the *main()*-function. In its only operation it initializes a new instance of the *WinMain*-class which will then overtake the user-interface-interaction.

A. Weber and S. Dustdar, *Haptic Systems Architecture Modeling*,
DOI 10.1007/978-3-7091-0755-3_4, © Springer-Verlag/Wien 2012

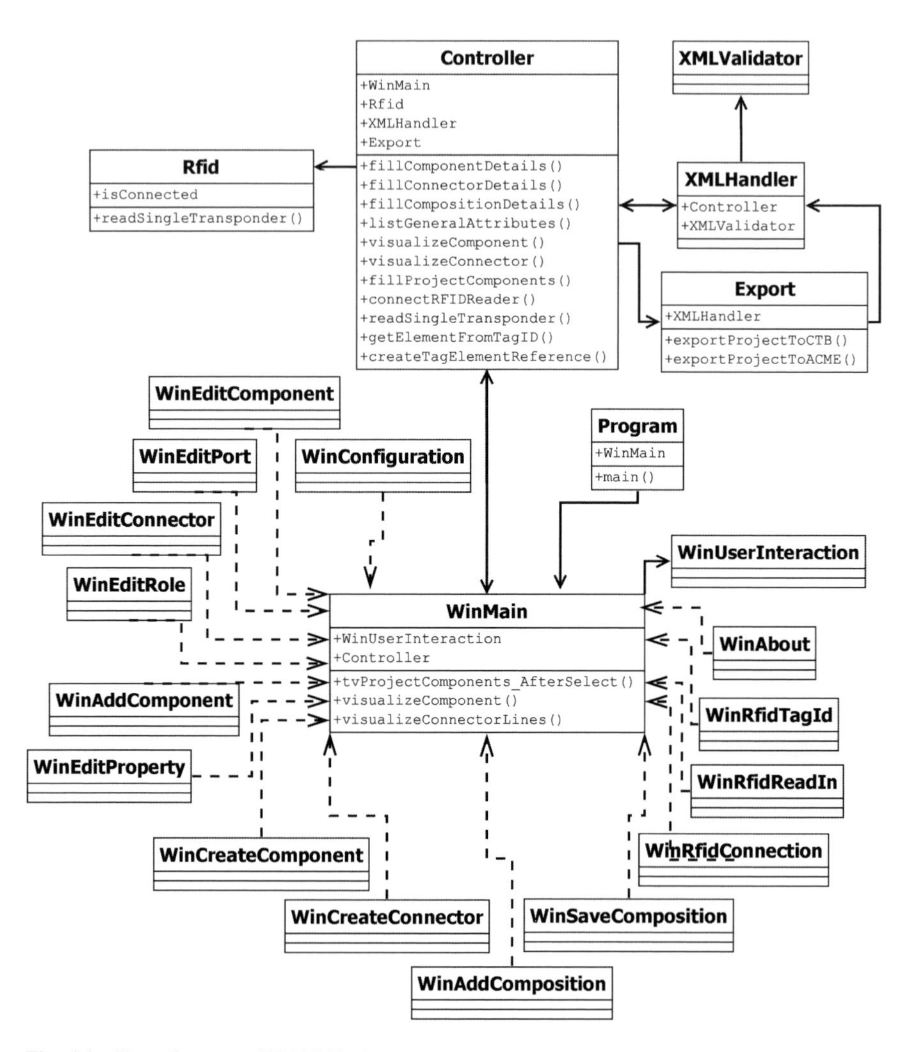

Fig. 4.1 Class diagram – HSAM-Tool

4.1.2 *Class: Controller*

The *Controller*-class is one of the most important classes for the HSAM-Tool. It provides numerous functions for the other classes to either access the user interfaces or vice versa the operating classes like *XMLHandler* or *Rfid*.

As its properties it holds amongst others instances of the classes *WinMain*, *XMLHandler*, *Rfid*, and *Export*.

4.1.2.1 Graphical-User-Interface Interaction

- *fillProjcectComponents()*
  - *Calling instance*: *Controller*, *WinMain*
  - *Functionality*: Determines all components, connectors, and compositions of the project and lists them in the *treeview*-section of the *WinMain*-instance.
- *fillComponentDetails()*
  - *Calling instance*: *WinMain*
  - *Functionality*: Determines all parameters of a component which was selected in the *WinMain*'s *treeview*-section, lists them in the *listview*-section, and calls for its visualization.
- *fillConnectorDetails()*
  - *Calling instance*: *WinMain*
  - *Functionality*: Determines all parameters of a connector which was selected in the *WinMain*'s *treeview*-section, lists them in the *listview*-section, and calls for its visualization.
- *fillCompositionDetails()*
  - *Calling instance*: *WinMain*
  - *Functionality*: Determines all parameters of a composition which was selected in the *WinMain*'s *treeview*-section and lists them in the *listview*-section.
- *listGeneralAttributes()*
  - *Calling instance*: *Controller*
  - *Functionality*: Determines all general attributes of the element which was selected in the *WinMain*'s *treeview*-section and lists them in the *listview*-section.
- *visualizeComponent()*
  - *Calling instance*: *Controller*
  - *Functionality*: Determines the picture of the selected component and paints it at a given point in the visualization-section of the *WinMain*-instance.
- *visualizeConnector()*
  - *Calling instance*: *Controller*
  - *Functionality*: Determines the picture of the selected connector, paints it at the middle of the visualization-section of the *WinMain*-instance, and calls for the visualization of the connector lines and of its components around its illustration.

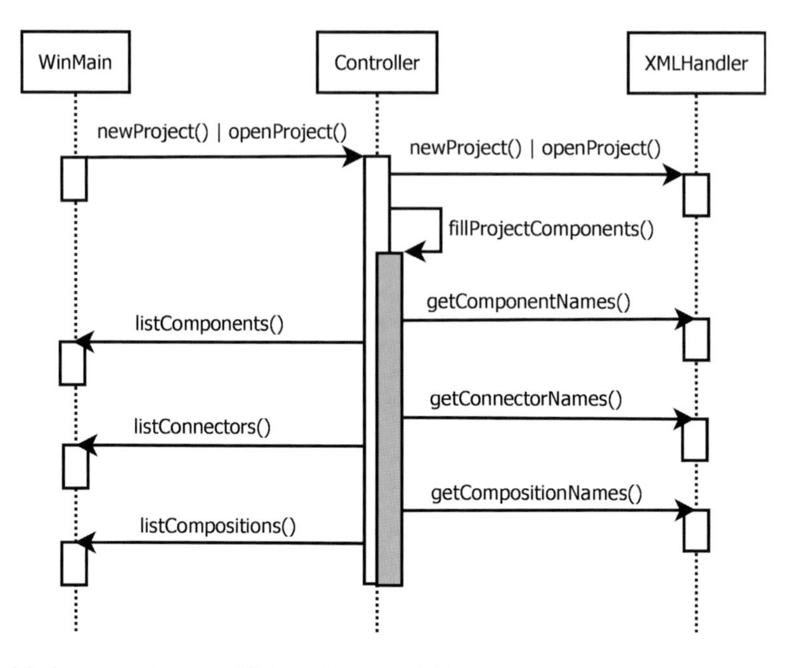

Fig. 4.2 Sequence diagram – *fillProjectComponents()*

Figure 4.2 shows a sequence diagram for calling the *fillProjectComponents()*-function in the *Controller*-class. This function is called whenever a project is created or opened, or when a component, connector, or composition is added to the current project.

It determines all components, connectors, and compositions of the current project. For each of the elements from those categories the function finds its information through the *XMLHandler* and writes it into the *listview*-section of the *WinMain*-instance.

Figure 4.3 shows a sequence diagram for the actions taken whenever an element in the *treeview*-section of the *WinMain*-instance is selected.

Depending on what kind of element was selected a different function in the controller is called. If the selected element is a component, the *fillComponentDetails ()*-function gets called. It determines the attributes and properties of the component, writes them into the *listview*-section of the *WinMain*-instance, and calls the *visualize-Component()*-function in the *WinMain*-class to let the component be painted in the middle of the visualization-section.

In case of a connector as the selected element, the *fillConnectorDetails()*-functions gets executed. It determines the attributes of the connector and writes them into the *listview*-section of the *WinMain*-instance. After that it calls the *visualizeConnector()*-function to paint the illustration of the connector in the middle of the visualization-section, surrounded by connection lines. Then it calls

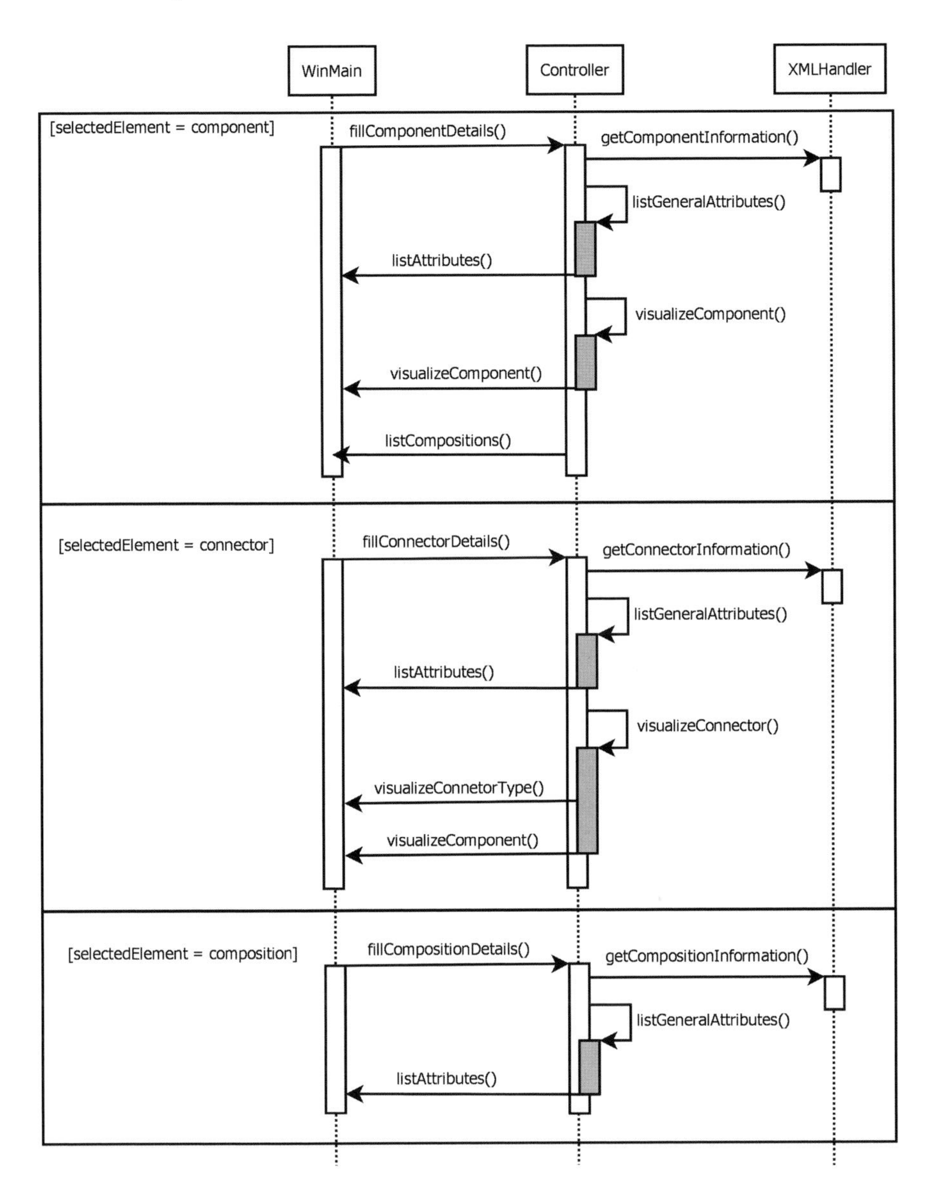

Fig. 4.3 Sequence diagram – *afterSelection()*

the *visualizeComponent()*-function for each component connected through the selected connector to paint it at the end of a connection line.

If the selected element in the *treeview* is a composition, the *fillCompositionDetails()*-function is called. It simply determines the attributes and included elements of the composition and lists them in the *listview*-section of the *WinMain*-instance.

4.1.2.2 RFID Interaction

– *connectRFIDReader()*
  - *Calling instance*: *WinRfidConnection*
  - *Functionality*: Determines baud-rate and protocol for RFID-reader and calls to open a connection to it.
– *disconnectRFIDReader()*
  - *Calling instance*: WinRfidConnection, Controller
  - *Functionality*: Determines if connection to RFID-reader exists and, if so, calls appropriate functions to disconnect it.
– *readSingleTransponder()*
  - *Calling instance*: Controller, WinRfidReadIn, WinRfidTagID, WinConfiguration
  - *Functionality*: Calls for the ID of a single transponder in range of the RFID-reader if a reader is connected.
– *getElementFromTagID()*
  - *Calling instance*: *WinRfidReadIn*
  - *Functionality*: Determines the referred element of a tag which was read in and creates the corresponding connector or component.
– *createTagElementReference()*
  - *Calling instance*: *WinRfidTagID*
  - *Functionality*: Creates a reference from a specific RFID-tag to an element-type.

Figure 4.4 shows a sequence diagram which illustrates the creation of the tag-element reference when the Lego element representations are tagged.

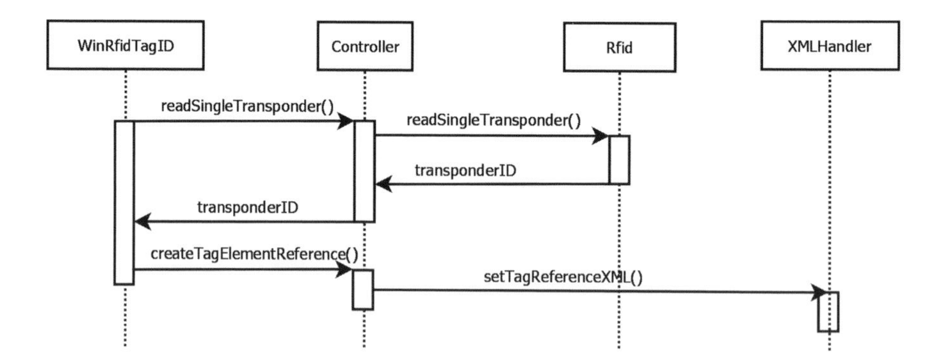

Fig. 4.4 Sequence diagram – *createTagElementReference()*

The class *WinRFIDTagID* which provides the graphical user interface to reference an element to a tag calls the *Controller*-function *readSingleTransponder()*. This in turn lets the *Controller* call the *readSingleTransponder()*-function from the *Rfid*-class. It returns the ID of a transponder placed directly in front of the reader and so the *createTagElementReference()*-function can be called. Through this function the *Controller*-class causes the *XMLHandler*-class to establish the reference by calling some provided operations.

In Fig. 4.5, the sequence diagram of calling the *getElementFromTagID()*-function of the Controller-instance is illustrated.

To do so, again the ID of a transponder is read and given to the *Controller*-function which determines its representing type with the help of the *XMLHandler*-class. If the type represents a connector, a new connector from this type is created if it does not already exist and the *treeview*-section in the *WinMain*-instance is updated. If the type is a component, first the controller needs to find out if the component was already created and if it is already connected to the current connector. If not, the new component is created and connected.

4.1.3 Class: WinMain

The class *WinMain* provides the most important graphical user interface which is the main window. In it the project's components are listed, their attributes are shown, and visualizations of components and connectors are painted. Moreover it is the class which creates, destructs, and delegates the other interfaces.

It provides functions of the Controller-instance to the other interfaces by holding it as a property. The second important property is of the kind *WinUserInteraction*.

- *tvProjectsComponents_AfterSelect()*
  - *Calling instance*: *WinMain*
  - *Functionality*: Handles the event which occurs when the selection in the treeview-section is altered.
- *visualizeComponent()*
  - *Calling instance*: *Controller*
  - *Functionality*: Visualizes an image of the selected element in the *treeview*-section in the middle or at a specific location within the visualization-section.
- *visualizeConnectorLines()*
  - *Calling instance*: *Controller*
  - *Functionality*: Visualizes the connecting lines of a connector-element selected in the *treeview*-section shaped like a star surrounding the center of the visualization-section.

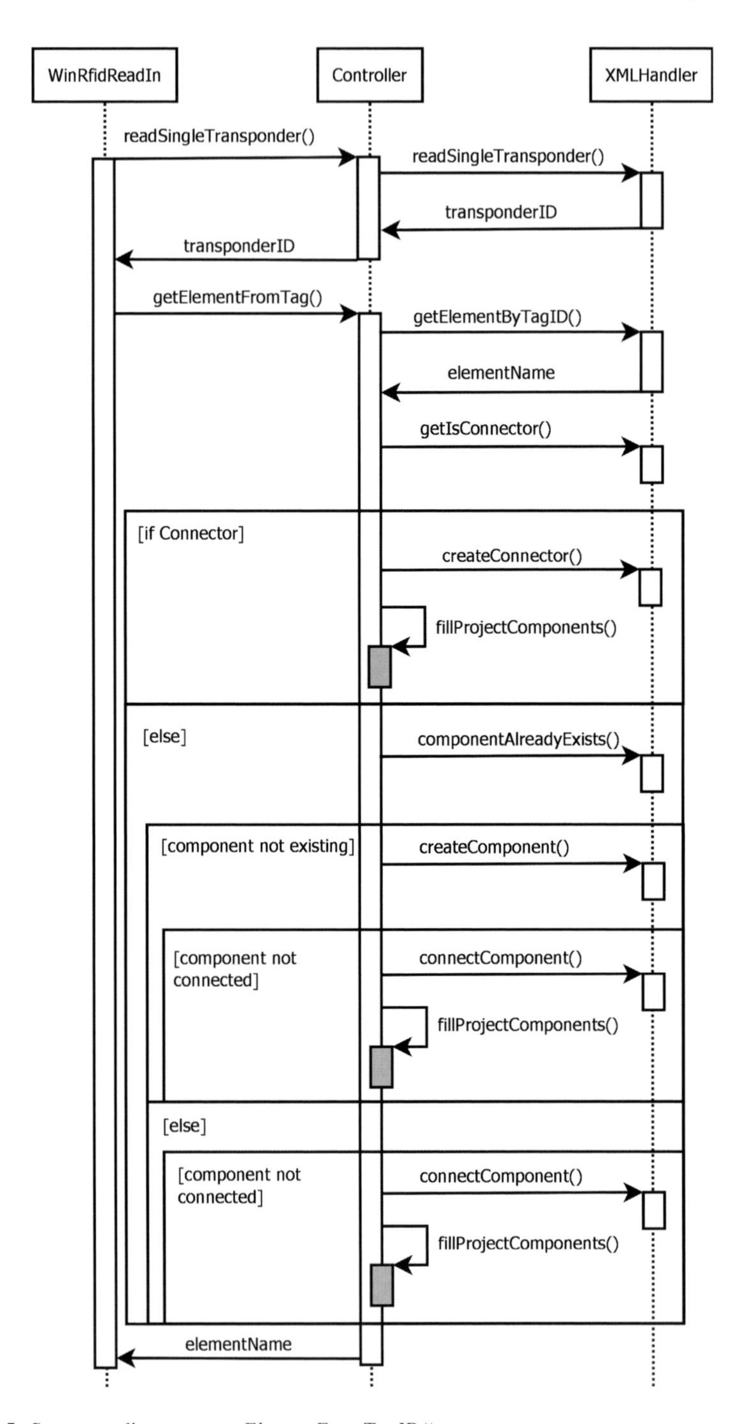

Fig. 4.5 Sequence diagram – *getElementFromTagID()*

4.1.4 Class: XMLHandler

The *XMLHandler*-class provides functionality to interact with the configuration and project xml-files. Those include creation of various nodes, editing of the node's content, providing the node's content, and deleting nodes.

The only important property to mention is the *XMLValidation*-instance.

4.1.5 Class: Export

An instance of the *Export*-class provides all functionalities to export a project to the ADL ACME or to CTB.

To gain access to xml-functionalities it holds an instance of the *XMLHandler*-class as a property.

– *exportProjectToACME()*
  - *Calling instance*: *Controller*
  - *Functionality*: Creates an acme-file and writes the converted project into it.
– *exportProjectToCTB()*
  - *Calling instance*: *Controller*
  - *Functionality*: Creates a ctb-file and writes the converted project into it.

4.1.6 Class: RFID

The RFID-class provides the functionality to gain access to a RFID-reader and to read the ID from a single transponder which is held directly in front of the reader. In order to correctly operate the reader, it wraps some functions provided by the library of ACG.[1]

It holds the variable *isConnected* as a property to provide the status of a connection to a RFID-reader to other classes.

– *readSingleTransponder()*
  - *Calling instance*: *Controller*
  - *Functionality*: Determines the ID of a RFID-transponder in range of the reader.

[1] ACG ID.

4.1.7 Other Classes

The following lists the rest of the defined classes which are shown in the class diagram and provides a brief description of them.

- *WinUserInteraction*
  Provides various inquiry call functions
- *WinAbout*
  Provides an information window about the HSAM-Tool
- *WinRfidTagId*
  Provides GUI to reference transponder-IDs to elements
- *WinRfidReadIn*
  Provides GUI to read in transponder-IDs
- *WinRfidConnection*
  Provides GUI to establish and dissolve connection to RFID-reader
- *WinSaveComposition*
  Provides GUI to save current project as a composition into the configuration-xml
- *WinCreateComponent*
  Provides GUI to add a component to the current project
- *WinCreateConnector*
  Provides GUI to add a connector to the current project
- *WinAddComposition*
  Provides GUI to add a composition of the configuration-xml to the current project
- *WinEditComponent*
  Provides GUI to edit a component
- *WinEditPort*
  Provides GUI to edit a port of a component
- *WinEditConnector*
  Provides GUI to edit a connector
- *WinEditRole*
  Provides GUI to edit a role of a connector
- *WinAddComponent*
  Provides GUI to add a component to a connector
- *WinEditProperty*
  Provides GUI to edit a property
- *WinConfiguration*
  Provides GUI to configure the HSAM-Tool
- *XMLValidator*
  Provides functionalities to validate the project and configuration-xmls (not used)

4.2 XML-Format

There are two kinds of XML-files relevant for the HSAM-Tool. First, there is the Configuration-XML. It provides a lot of relevant information which can be altered without rebuilding the program.

Second, there are the project-XMLs. They are generated and expanded whenever a project is created and edited and their file is stored when the project is saved.

4.2.1 Configuration-XML

The configuration-XML consists of a root node called Config. It provides the main information on the project as attributes. The attribute value HSAM-Config.xsd references to scheme with which the configuration-XML can be validated.

```
<Config xml-version="1.0" xsi:noNamespaceSchemaLocation="HSAM-Config.xsd">
```

The Config-node only holds the children Components, Compositions, and Program. Components holds a list of all Component-nodes which later can be created in the HSAM-Tool. The Compositions-node features a list of all Composition-nodes which are created over the time. The Program-node holds some properties relevant to the program itself and to some margin values.

The following is an example for a Component-node:

```
<Component name="Client" description="it's a client" connector="false">
  <Properties>
    <Property name="picPath" type="string" value="client.gif"
      required="false" />
    <Property name="physicalComponent" type="string" value="unspecified"
      required="true" />
    <Property name="executionEnvironment" type="string"
      value="unspecified" required="true" />
    <Property name="application" type="string" value="unspecified"
      required="true" />
    <Property name="CPU" type="integer" value="" required="true" />
    <Property name="RAM" type="integer" value="" required="true" />
    <Property name="HD" type="integer" value="" required="true" />
    <Property name="OS" type="string" value="" required="true" />
    <Property name="Constraint" type="OCL" value="" required="true" />
  </Properties>
</Component>
```

As attributes it features the components name, description, and the flag connector which describes the component as a connecting component or not. This is relevant for the construction of the system because non-connecting components can only be connected to connecting components and vice versa. Each Component-node needs to hold a Properties-node which again needs to hold a Property-node with an attribute name whose value is picPath.

This is because else there will be no visualization of the component for the project. Its attribute `required` flags the property if it will be added to the element when it is created and added to a project. In addition any other `Property`-node added to the element will be a potential default property for the element depending on its `required` attribute. For the example above, the element will receive the properties `CPU`, `RAM`, `HD`, `OS`, and `Constraint` whenever it is created.

Physical-component	Execution-environment	Application	Network	Property-types
Unspecified	Unspecified	Unspecified	Unspecified	String
MobileDevice	MidletContainer	Database	Internet	Integer
Workstation	ApplicationContainer	DirectoryService	Intranet	Float
OfficeServer	ServletContainer	MessagingSystem	LAN	Boolean
Mainframe	ApplicationServer	EventBroker		OCL
ExternalSystem	GenericContainer	GroupwareServer		Undefined
GenericDevice	PortletContainer	DirectoryServer		
	LightweightContainer	ObjectRequestBroker		
	AppletContainer	WebServer		
	CDCContainer	MailServer		
		PortalServer		
		PresentationServer		
		EnterpriseServiceBus		
		DistributedTransaction-Management		
		Cache		
		LoadBalancer		
		UDDIServer		
		RuleBasedEngine		
		PushSystem		
		WebBrowser		
		MailClient		
		Firewall		

The `Composition`-node is actually made up like a project. So see the next subchapter for explanation. The only additional information is an `id` to be able to properly identify the composition.

The `Program`-node features some `Property`-nodes to provide some variables for the program. If changed in the XML, they surly influence the program. It also holds a `VariableValues`-node. This node again holds the nodes `Physical-Component`, `ExecutionEnvironment`, `Application`, `Network`, and `PropertyTypes`. They each feature a list of children whose node-names define the approved values for the variables called like their node name. They can be either defined to provide a smooth export–import to the Component Toolbox or to provide a range of values a variable can be assigned to. Predefined values are listed in the above table.

```
<Program>
  <Properties>
    <Property name="lineColor" value="Blue" description="Color of Connector-
      Lines; Have to be named as described in C# Color-Class specification" />
    <Property name="lineLength" value="285" description="Length of
      Connector-Lines; If blank forth of width of window is used" />
    <Property name="lineThickness" value="3" description="Thickness of
      Connector-Lines" />
    <Property name="picPath" value="/data/" description="Path to Component-
      Visualizations; relative to Path of Program">
    </Property>
    <Property name="baudRate" value="9600" description="Baud Rate for RFID-
      Reader" />
    <Property name="protocol" value="0" description="Protocol for RFID-
      Reader" />
  </Properties>
  <VariableValues>
    <physicalcomponent />
    <executionenvironment />
    <application />
    <network />
    <PropertyTypes />
  </VariableValues>
</Program>
```

4.2.2 Project-XML

A project-XML always consists of a root node called `Project`. It provides the main information on the project as attributes. The attribute value `HSAM.xsd` references to the scheme with which the project-XML can be validated.

```
<Project xml-version="1.0" name="ClientServer" author="Tony" date="09.10.2007
  14:15:35" xmlns:xsi="http://www.w3.org/2001/XMLSchema-instance"
  xsi:noNamespaceSchemaLocation="HSAM.xsd">
```

The only child nodes it holds are `Properties`, `Components`, `Connectors`, `Compositions`, and `TransponderIDs`, each of which holds `Property-`, `Component-`, `Connector-`, `Composition-`, or `TransponderID`-child nodes. The child nodes of `Properties` holds properties defined for the whole project. However, their layout and designation fits the `Property`-nodes shown in the next example. A typical `Component` node looks like this:

```
<Component name="client1" type="client" description="" id="client1">
  <Properties>
    <Property name="physicalComponent" type="string" value="unspecified"
      meta="invisible" />
    <Property name="executionEnvironment" type="string"
      value="unspecified" meta="invisible" />
    <Property name="application" type="string" value="unspecified"
      meta="invisible" />
    <Property name="CPU" type="integer" value="" meta="invisible" />
    <Property name="RAM" type="integer" value="" meta="invisible" />
    <Property name="HD" type="integer" value="" meta="invisible" />
    <Property name="OS" type="string" value="" meta="invisible" />
    <Property name="Constraint" type="OCL" value="" meta="invisible" />
  </Properties>
  <Ports>
    <Port name="defaultPort" description="Default Port" id="client1_port1">
      <Properties>
        <Property name="Constraint" type="OCL" value="" meta="" />
      </Properties>
    </Port>
  </Ports>
</Component>
```

It contains a Properties-node which holds all Property-nodes of the component. They always feature the attributes name, type, value, and meta. The meta-attribute defines if the property will be exported to CTB when the project is exported. This is useful to differ between such properties which are specific for HSAM and such properties which are needed for importing the project to CTB. Moreover, the Component holds a list of all Ports which again features some main attributes, as well as a list of relevant Properties.

A typical Connector-node looks like the following:

```
<Connector name="con1" type="internet" description="" id="con1">
  <Properties>
    <Property name="Constraint" type="OCL" value="" meta="invisible" />
    <Property name="TransportProtocol" type="string" value=""
      meta="invisible" />
    <Property name="Max_Bandwidth_mb" type="integer" value=""
      meta="invisible" />
  </Properties>
  <Roles>
    <Role name="defaultRole" description="" port_ref="server1_port1"
      id="con1_role1">
      <Properties>
        <Property name="Constraint" type="OCL" value="" meta="" />
      </Properties>
    </Role>
    <Role name="defaultRole" description="" port_ref="client1_port1"
      id="con1_role2">
      <Properties>
        <Property name="Constraint" type="OCL" value="" meta="" />
      </Properties>
     </Role>
  </Roles>
</Connector>
```

Also the Connector holds a Properties-node which follows the same rules as the ones in the Component-node. Instead of Ports, the Connector-node features a Roles-node which holds the Role-nodes. Notice that a Role-node references to a Port-node through the attribute port_ref. This is how connections between components are defined.

At last, there is a typical Composition-node. It only features an attribute which references to a Composition-node in the configuration-XML:

```
<Composition composition_ref="composition1"/>
```

A typical TranspnderID-node looks like the following:

```
<TransponderID elementType="client" transponderID="F639E6B8"
  elementID="client1" />
```

It provides the reference between a specific transponder and a type of element. The attribute elementType holds the type of element, trasponderID refers to the ID of the transponder, and elementID holds a key of an element when a reference was established.

4.3 Export-Format

The HSAM-Tool provides two formats to export a project to. How the export functions are reached is shown in Sect. 4.4.

The first export format is the code of the ADL ACME. A file is generated when exporting the project into ACME which holds the definitions of each component and their connection to each other. Refer to the ABLE[2] homepage for further information on the ACME code.

The second exportation format is more important due to the fact that its importing program was developed specifically for it. The outcome is of the format *ctb-xml*, which refers to the name of the importing program, namely "Component Toolbox", and which was introduced by Hofstetter.[3]

This program provides full compatibility to the exported projects and features a modeling tool to design software architecture based on the imported system structure.

The following example shows a simple client–server-connection through the internet.

```
<?xml version="1.0" encoding="UTF-8"?>
<ctb:Diagram xmi:version="2.0" xmlns:xmi="http://www.omg.org/XMI"
  xmlns:xsi="http://www.w3.org/2001/XMLSchema-instance"
  xmlns:ctb="http://ctb.com">
  <physicalComponents xsi:type="ctb:PhysicalComponent" Typ="unspecified" />
  <physicalComponents xsi:type="ctb:PhysicalComponent" Typ="unspecified" />
  <networks />
  <networkConnections targetNetwork="//@networks.0"
```

The root element is `ctb:Diagram` with its attributes of version and namespaces of `xmi`, `xsi`, and `ctb`. It can hold three different child-nodes which are `physicalComponents`, `networks`, and `networkConnections`.

The nodes `physicalComponents` represent the components in the HSAM-Tool. In order for the tool to correctly interact with the Component Toolbox it adds default child-nodes `executionEnvironments` and `runtimeComponents` to a component when exported to CTB. In the HSAM-Tool the values of their attribute `Typ` can be chosen from a defined pool shown in Sect. 4.2.1.

The nodes `networks` define the connectors of a system architecture. They do not feature any attributes due to incompatibility.

The last type of child-nodes is `networkConnections`. These nodes define the actual connection of a component to a connector provided by ports and roles in the HSAM-Tool. They feature two attributes which are `targetNetwork` and `sourceComponent`. As the names of the attributes already reveal, a component is always connected to a connector, but not to another component neither is a connector directly connected to another connector.

Other properties of elements defined in the HSAM-Tool are not exported to CTB due to incompatibility of the unknown property-types.

---

[2] ABLE – Architecture Based Languages and Environments 2007.

[3] Hofstetter 2007.

4.4 Graphical User Interfaces

The following list shows how to reach various functions in the HSAM-Tool:

Command	Result	Accessibility
Create project	Creates a new project	File → New project
Open project	Opens an existing project	File → Open project
Save project	Saves an opened project at its location	File → Save project
Save project as	Saves an opened project under a new filename	File → Save project as
Save as composition	Saves an opened project as a composition into the config-xml	File → Save as composition
Close project	Closes an opened project	File → Close project
Read in architecture	Opens GUI to read in an architecture	Project → Read in architecture
Tag architecture elements	Opens GUI to reference transponders to elements	Project → Tag architecture elements
Connect RFID reader	Opens GUI to connect and disconnect to RFID reader	Project → Connect RFID reader
Export to ACME	Exports an opened project to ACME code	Project → Export to ACME
Export to CTB	Exports an opened project to CTB-XML	Project → Export to CTB
Project properties	Opens a dialog to configure the project's properties	Project → Project properties
Create component	Adds a new component to the opened project	(In component section of the tool strip)
Delete component	Deletes a component from the opened project	
Create connector	Adds a new connector to the opened project	(In connector section of the tool strip)
Delete connector	Deletes a connector from the opened project	
Create composition	Adds a new composition to the opened project	(In composition section of the tool strip)
Delete composition	Deletes a composition from the opened project	
Options	Opens the options dialog	Extras → Options
Exit program	Exits the program	File → Exit

4.4.1 Main Window

The main window is presented right at the start of the HSAM-Tool. It is the center of the tool presenting all of a project's contents (Fig. 4.6).

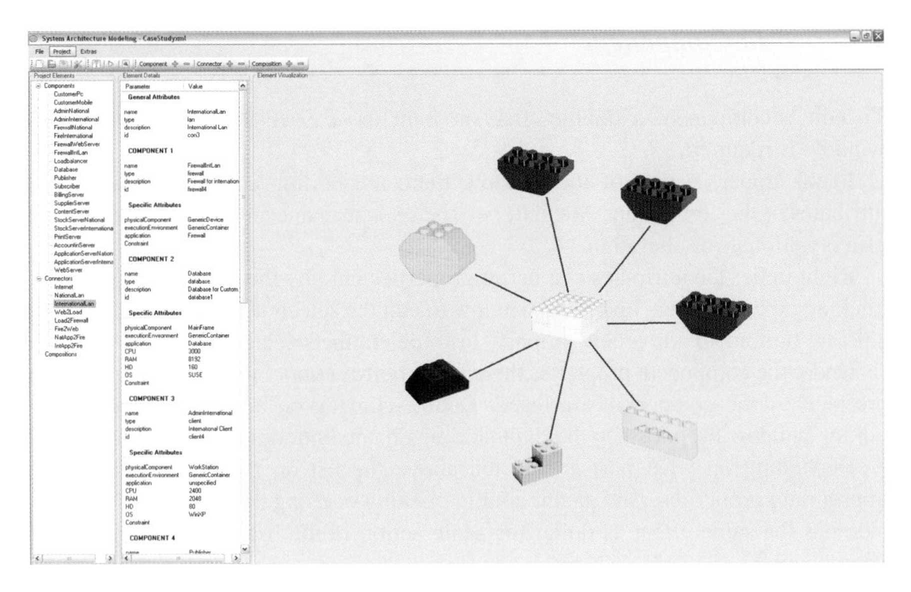

Fig. 4.6 Screenshot – main window

On the top of the window the menu-bar is situated. It provides access to most of the functions the tool offers as shown in the list above. Beneath is a breakdown of three areas. The first one on the left holds a tree-view which shows all components, connectors, and compositions of an opened project. In the middle there is a list which provides information on an element when it is selected on the left. And on the right there is room for the visualization of the selected element. Hovering the mouse over one of the pictures lets appear information about its element.

In order to reach the RFID- and project-specific-functionalities, like exportation, a project needs to be opened or created first. In addition to the RFID-operations, first a reader needs to be connected to the tool using the appropriate commands.

To reach the editing windows of components and connectors a double-click on the according element in the left section is required.

4.4.2 Save As Composition

Saving a project as composition enables its elements to be imported as a whole later on to other projects. It will be saved in the configuration-xml at its compositions-section.

To reach the dialogue a project needs to be opened, and to save it as a composition a name is required to identify it later on. Optionally, a description can be added which later helps the user to decide which composition to import.

4.4.3 Edit Component

To edit a component a double-click on it in the *treeview*-section of the main window is required.

In the upper section of the window there are editing controls for the main attributes of the component. Mandatory to be set is its name and its type. Everything else is optional for alteration.

Right under the attributes is a list of properties held by the component. Double-clicking on one of them opens the window to edit the selected property. On the right side are buttons to add a new property or to delete the selected one.

Under the component properties there is the port-section. First, all the ports which are held by the component are listed. Double-clicking on one of them opens the editing window for ports. On the right side, again, are buttons to add or delete a port.

Depending on what port is selected above the list on the bottom shows the appropriate properties. And again, double-clicking or using the buttons on the right side has the same effect as doing the same action in the list of properties for the component.

4.4.4 Edit Port/Add Port

To edit a port first the editing window of a component has to be opened to then double-click on a port listed in its ports-section.

The name and description of a port can be altered whereas a value for the name is mandatory in order to save the alterations.

4.4.5 Edit Connector

Opening the connector editing window is done by double-clicking on a connector in the *treeview*-section of the main window.

As for the component editing window, the connector editing window first provides controls to alter its name, type, and description. Again, as for the component, name and type are mandatory to save the connector.

Beneath is the list of held properties. Double-clicking on one of them opens the property editing window. On the right side there are buttons to add or delete a property.

Under the properties is the listing of the connection to components featured by the connector. It shows the component's name, type, description, and the port the connector is connecting to. Double-clicking on one of the components opens its editing window. The buttons on the right allow deleting or adding a connection to the connector.

The next section is the list of roles the connector holds by providing connections to components. They can be edited by double-clicking on one of them, added by adding a new component to the connector, and deleted by deleting the appropriate component which also deletes the connection between the component and the connector.

The lowest section holds the list of role properties according to the selected role above. As for the other property listings, double-clicking opens the editing window and using the buttons on the right adds or deletes a property to or of the selected role.

4.4.6 Add Component to Connector/Edit Role

To add a component to a connector means to establish a connection between them and to create a role for the connector which references to a port of the component.

This window can be reached by pressing the *add*-button on the right side of the *components*-list or by double-clicking on one of the roles in the *roles*-section in the *connector editing* window.

First, the dialogue shows controls for the name and description of the role the connector holds or is about to if adding a connection. Under those there are two *comboboxes*. The one on the left provides a listing of all components included in the project. The second holds the ports which are featured by the component selected in the first *combobox*.

Depending on how the window was reached values may be entered in the provided controls. However, a name for the role, a component, and the component's port are mandatory to save the alterations.

If a new role was created and saved correctly, then also a connection between the connector and the selected component was created using the selected port. The connector holds this new role which possesses a reference to this port as a node in the project xml-file.

4.4.7 Add/Edit Property

There are two ways of reaching this dialogue. First the *add*-buttons on the right side of any *properties* listing opens it with no values assigned to the controls. The second way is to double-click to a general property in such a listing, whereby now the controls feature the values of the property which are name, type, value, and visibility.

Altering or choosing the type of the property means to alter the type of value the property holds. However, the correctness of the value according to its type is not guaranteed by the HSAM-Tool.

The visibility attribute of the property is responsible to decide whether the property will be considered when the project is exported or not.

All controls need to be filled with a value to save the property successfully.

4.4.8 Edit Special Property

Special properties are those which feature a single type of value and only a defined range of values which can be assigned to the property.

This dialogue opens after double-clicking on a special property is performed.

The only way to add a special property to an element is to add it as a default property by appending it to the appropriate parent-node in the configuration xml-file. Then the range of values needs to be defined in the *variables*-section of the configuration xml.

Again, all controls need to hold values in order to save the alterations.

4.4.9 Add Component/Connector to Project

This window appears when clicking on the buttons to add a component or connector located in the *menustrip* of the main window.

For both elements the dialogue looks the same but the outcome is a different one. Depending on which button was pressed the dialogue creates the according element for the current project when saved successfully.

To do so a name and type of the element needs to be provided. The description is optional.

4.4.10 Add Composition to Project

To reach this dialogue a click on the appropriate button located in the *menustrip* of the main window is required.

It allows the user to add a whole composition to the current project. This composition needs to be saved into the configuration xml-file prior to the importation to the current project.

Selecting an existing composition is necessary to save the alteration. To help the user decide, the lower text labels hold additional information on the composition selected in the upper *combobox*.

When a composition is imported, all its components, connectors, and compositions are added to the current project.

4.4.11 Open Reader Connection

This window is reached by clicking on the right button in the *menustrip* of the main window.

It allows the user to establish a connection to a RFID-reader or to dissolve an existing one.

In order to connect to a reader if no connection exists, the right COM-port needs to be chosen. In the next step, it can be tried to establish the connection by clicking on the *open reader*-button. If the connection process is successful, information on the connected reader is shown. Otherwise, the user gets prompted to choose the right port.

If the dialogue is opened while a connection to a reader exists, the user can close the connection by clicking on the *close reader*-button.

4.4.12 Refer Tag IDs

The dialogue to reference transponder IDs to specific element types can only be accessed when a connection to a RFID-reader exists.

In order to establish such a reference, the user is asked to choose a type of element that he wants to be referenced by the tag. Then he places a transponder right in front of the reader as shown in Fig. 3.2 to then hit the *tag*-button. If the establishing process is successful, appropriate information will be shown in the *information*-section of the window.

Referring a tag to multiple types of elements only stores the last executed one. The reference itself will be stored in the project xml-file. Refer to Sect. 4.2.2 for more information.

4.4.13 Read in Elements

As for the *refer tag IDs*-dialogue, there needs to be an established connection to a RFID-reader before opening the *read in elements*-dialogue.

If a connection exists, a tag which is placed directly in front of the RFID-reader as shown in Fig. 3.2 can be read in. There will be feedback for the user according to the status of the read in process. This feedback includes information on whether a tag is found and a reference using this tag exists, or a tag is found and no reference for this tag exists, or the tag is not found at all.

However, there is one constraint the user has to follow in order to read in an architecture successfully. Due to the way the HSAM-Tool handles the connections between components and connectors, there always needs to be a connector to be read in before reading in components. This is because otherwise a connection from a component to a connector could not be generated automatically. Refer to Sect. 3.3.2.1 for detailed information.

When reading in a referenced tag the appropriate element will be created in the background for the current project and, if the element is a component, connected to the prior read in connector.

4.4.14 Edit Project Properties

This window can only be accessed when a project is opened.

It lists the properties of the current project which can be edited by double-clicking on one of them. Adding or deleting a property is done by clicking on the according button on the right side of the list.

4.4.15 Configuration

This window provides controls to configure general attributes of the HSAM-Tool.

It is split into two major domains. The first one holds attributes for the visualization of a project's elements. The second one is for establishing a connection to a RFID-reader.

Most of the attributes can only be assigned to a defined range of values. However, the path for the element visualizations is, as well as the settings for the RFID-reader, set to operate in the used environment.

Saving the alterations edits the values in the configuration xml-file.

Chapter 5
Element Representations

In the following a list of fundamental elements needed to build a system architecture using HSAM is presented. The list does not claim completeness and can be expanded as desired. The basic elements were extracted from Dustdar[1] and Birkhölzer.[2]

5.1 Definitions

In this part the various Lego bricks and the way they will be referred to in the further document will be illustrated and described.

5.1.1 Lego-Parts Legend

Lego-parts are always described by three parameters. Those are height, length and width. In general the default height is the one of the classic Lego-brick as shown in Fig. 5.1. The height will be described by the terms "brick" and "plate". Table 5.1 shows the difference between those expressions. If a brick's height varies from these defaults it is mentioned explicitly.

The length and width of a brick is categorized by the number of studs on top of the brick. In case of the brick shown in Fig. 5.1 it is therefore called a 2 × 4-brick. The smaller number of both parameters is always placed first. Generally this is the width of the brick.

Table 5.1 shows most relevant bricks and plates. However, the table does not list the complete compendium of Lego-elements. Lego provides much more parts variable in size, color and shape. Of course such extra parts can also be used to define individual elements.

---

[1] Dustdar et al. 2003.

[2] Birkhölzer and Vaupel 2003.

A. Weber and S. Dustdar, *Haptic Systems Architecture Modeling*,
DOI 10.1007/978-3-7091-0755-3_5, © Springer-Verlag/Wien 2012

Fig. 5.1 Classic 2 × 4 Lego-brick

Table 5.1 Most important Lego-elements

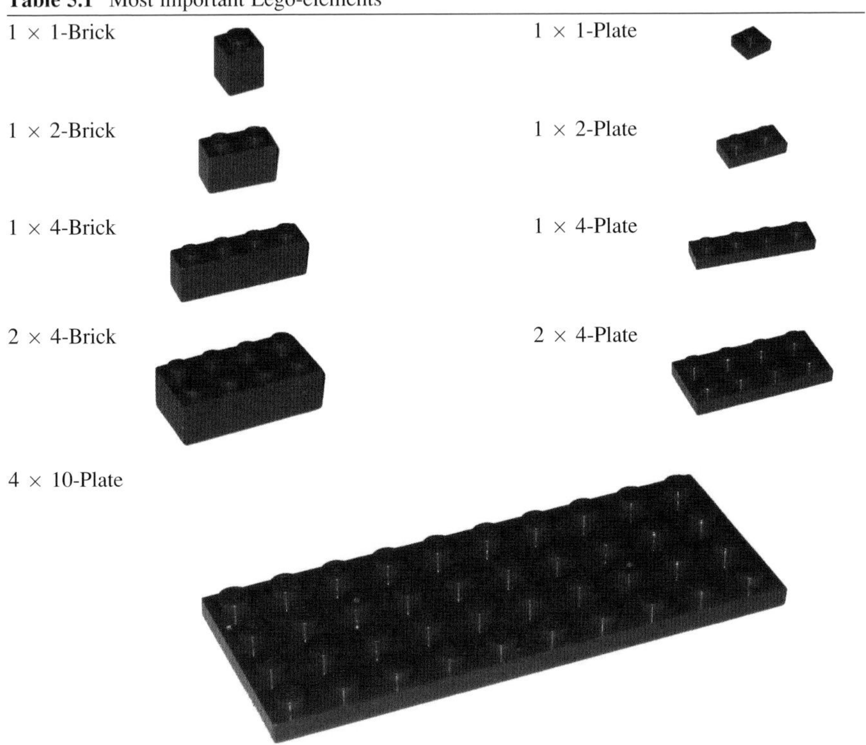

1 × 1-Brick	1 × 1-Plate
1 × 2-Brick	1 × 2-Plate
1 × 4-Brick	1 × 4-Plate
2 × 4-Brick	2 × 4-Plate
4 × 10-Plate	

5.1.2 *Building Instructions*

Lego-elements have to be stacked in their predetermined way. Different elements can be stacked on to each other to combine them. It is not allowed to misapply their studs or any other parts to balance them so that the result is an unstable construction. See Fig. 5.2 as example for a valid construction and Fig. 5.3 for a non valid construction example.

Two different Lego-parts are called "neighbors" when they are stacked to a pile or when they are right next to each other so that the Lego-building is still a valid construction.

When assembling various Lego-parts to a valid construction neighboring parts of the same color (see Figs. 5.4 and 5.5) are understood to be of the same basic building

Fig. 5.2 Valid Lego-construction

Fig. 5.3 None valid Lego-construction

Fig. 5.4 Non neighboring Lego-bricks

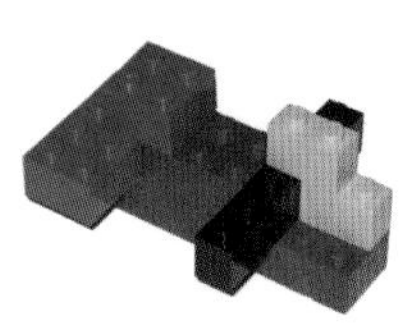

Fig. 5.5 Neighboring Lego-bricks

element as listed further below in this document. One exception is going to be the bricks holding the RFID-transponders. See Sect. 5.1.3 for further explanation.

Which Lego-bricks are used to build an element out of this catalogue is up to the constructor. It is not compulsory to use the bricks described for each element. However, the constraints for each element have to be followed.

5.1.3 RFID-Transponder Integration

Because the used RFID-transponders are not self-adhesive they need to be integrated into some Lego-bricks. Therefore some customization needs to take place.

5.1.3.1 Customize

The appointed bricks for holding the transponders are orange 2×4-bricks. Each transponder needs to be embedded into two such bricks. To do so cut open the top of the first and the bottom of the second brick (for this book a slotted screwdriver and a hammer was used) and carefully stick the transponder into the brick with the opened top. The result will be the bottom of the transponder-brick-construction. Then carefully attach the second brick with the opened bottom on top of the first brick making sure that the transponder slides into its opening so that the whole transponder will disappear in the center of those two bricks. The following array of illustrations will visualize the process of customization (Figs. 5.6–5.8).

5.1.3.2 Integrate

To integrate the transponder-bricks into the basic building elements simply attach the transponder-bricks to the bricks used for the elements. Because the transponder-bricks feature a unique color it is recommended to fully embed the bricks into the construction of the element so that it is surrounded at least at two sides. If that is not possible, then the construction of the element should be chosen in such a way that the attached transponder-bricks intuitively appear to belong to the element. However, in such a case the transponder-bricks are understood to belong and represent

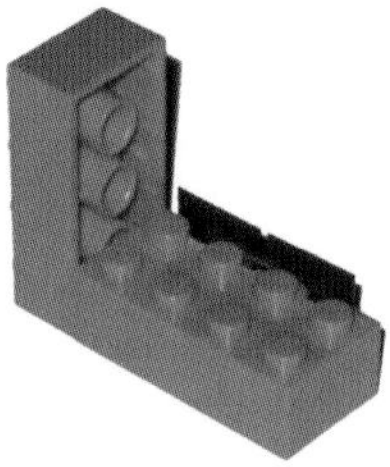

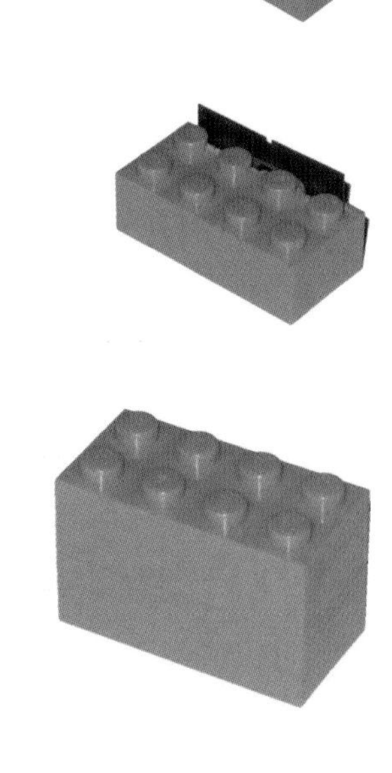

Fig. 5.6 Customized transponder bricks

Fig. 5.7 Lower brick holding transponder

Fig. 5.8 Full transponder integration

Fig. 5.9 Valid transponder brick integration

the element to which they are attached to. I.e. an attached transponder-brick which is only connected to its element on one side can feature another Lego-brick of the same color as the element requests at the opposite side and still appears to represent one single element. Figure 5.9 illustrates such an element. The transponder bricks are understood to be part of the whole element.

5.2 Catalogue of Elements

The basic elements are separated by classification of matter into the categories Networks, Client–Server, Publisher–Subscriber, Sender–Receiver, Master–Slave, Pipe–Filter, Database, Model-View-Controller, Protocols, Miscellaneous, and Meta elements.

Each element is described by an introduction including its characterization, a construction plan explaining how the element is built, and a value for being a connecting element or not. For those elements used in the case study later on a guideline of principles defining how the element can be applied, what meaning results of the way of its application, and what variations in building the element are allowed. However, the application principles are only valid for the case study presented in Chap. 6 but of course can also be adapted for further projects.

– *General variations*

For constructing reasons the shapes and sizes of all elements can differ from those shown in the following list. Often transparency is higher when elements of the same type differ in size, shape, location, and orientation.

More important elements can be built bigger or broader to indicate their importance. Variation in size can emphasize differences between elements of the same kind, e.g. a web server could be shaped differently than a mail server. Still both elements are servers and thus they need to obey the main idea of their shape. I.e. no matter how the elements can be altered and diversified in their appearance they still need to fulfill the requirements given by this catalogue.

Due to the neighboring rule elements are also allowed to feature special variations which first seem to violate the catalogues rules. E.g. a column can be added in order to guarantee the integration of the element into the rest of the construction (see case study in Chap. 6 for an example). Therefore such special variations need to be limited enough so that the element can still be interpreted as an element of its kind.

5.2.1 Networks

Elements in this group mostly represent a whole network. There are only router and firewall to which this does not apply. If elements of this group occur in the same project the Lego compositions of larger networks should be built larger than the ones of smaller networks. This is because the size can already indicate the type of network the representation stands for.

5.2.1.1 Backbone

Backbones connect autonomous lower-level networks so that they can exchange information (Fig. 5.10).[3]

Construction

- Color: Grey
- Layout: The backbone-element is built like a ring with the height of at least two Lego-bricks. The length of the ring has to include at least four Lego-bricks.
- Kind: Connector

5.2.1.2 Internet

The internet is the well known combination of so many sub-networks distributed all over the world. It is decentralized and therefore not subdued to any specific instance (Fig. 5.11).[4,5]

Fig. 5.10 Backbone

[3] Broy and Spaniol 1999.
[4] Broy and Spaniol 1999.
[5] Klußmann 2000.

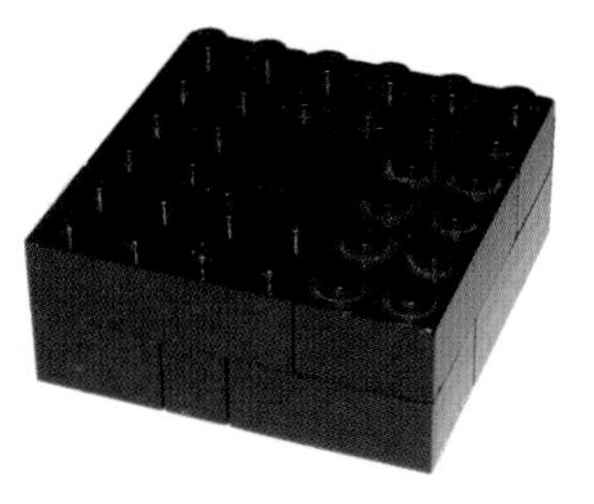

Fig. 5.11 Internet

Fig. 5.12 Intranet

Construction

- Color: Black
- Layout: The internet-element is built like a ring with the height of at least two Lego-bricks. The length of the ring has to include at least four Lego-bricks.
- Kind: Connector

Principles of Application

The size of the constructions indicates the size of the actual network. Therefore the internet should be built the biggest of all networking elements.

5.2.1.3 Intranet

The big difference between Internet and Intranet is that within the Intranet all attached components can be trusted. Therefore Intranets are only operated by companies or other corporate bodies (Fig. 5.12).[6]

Construction

- Color: Blue
- Layout: The Intranet-element is built like a ring with the height of at least two Lego-bricks. The length of the ring has to include at least four Lego-bricks.
- Kind: Connector

[6] Broy and Spaniol 1999.

Principles of Application

The intranet is only used for simple connections between other elements. Therefore no special variation is needed. It is built the smallest way to indicate no special meanings. However, in the case study it features a special variation. Two 2×2 bricks are attached on top of the intranet in order to provide a solid construction.

5.2.1.4 Local Area Network (LAN)

The LAN-element represents networks within the range of 10 km. Mostly they are spread within buildings or organizations (Fig. 5.13).[7]

Construction

- Color: White
- Layout: The LAN-element is built like a ring with the height of at least two Lego-bricks. The circumference of the ring has to include at least four Lego-bricks.
- Kind: Connector

Principles of Application

Its circumference is an indication for how many elements can be connected to the LAN. Longer circumferences therefore indicate a bigger LAN.

5.2.1.5 Metropolitan Area Network (MAN)

The MAN-element represents networks within the range of 20 km. Its characteristics are its situation in an urban area and its range of high data rates (Fig. 5.14).[8]

Fig. 5.13 LAN

[7] Klußmann 2000.

[8] Klußmann 2000.

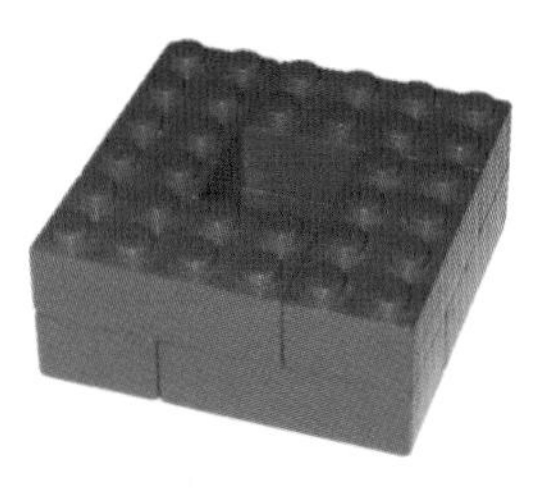

Fig. 5.14 MAN

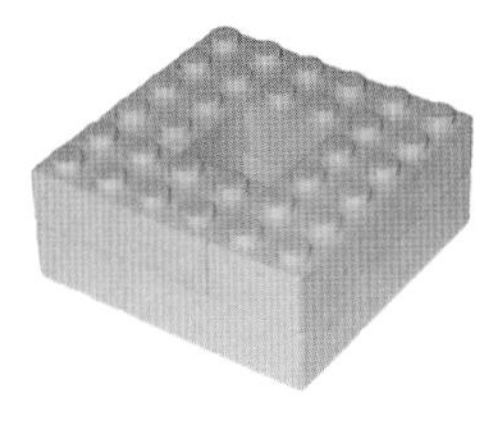

Fig. 5.15 WAN

Construction

- Color: Red
- Layout: The MAN-element is built like a ring with the height of at least two Lego-bricks. The length of the ring has to include at least four Lego-bricks.
- Kind: Connector

5.2.1.6 Wide Area Network (WAN)

The WAN-element represents networks with a range of more than 10 km. Often it provides backbone-like functionality (Fig. 5.15).[9]

Construction

- Color: Yellow
- Layout: The WAN-element is built like a ring with the height of at least two Lego-bricks. The length of the ring has to include at least four Lego-bricks.
- Kind: Connector

5.2.1.7 Storage Area Network (SAN)

According to Tate a SAN is a type of network which main eligibility is to transfer data between computing elements and storing elements (Fig. 5.16).

[9] Klußmann 2000.

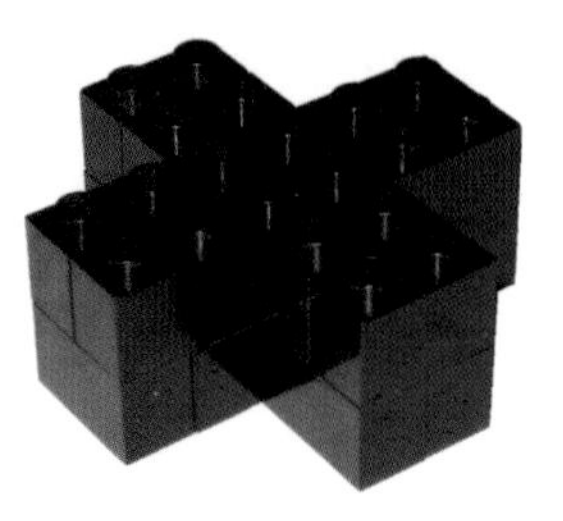

Fig. 5.16 SAN

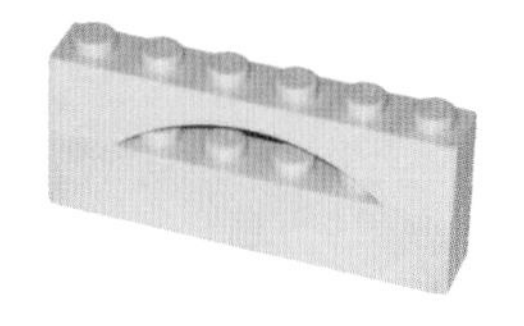

Fig. 5.17 Firewall

> A SAN can also be a storage system consisting of storage elements, storage devices, computer systems, and/or appliances, plus all control software, communicating over a network.[10]

Construction

- Color: Black
- Layout: The shape for the element for SAN is a cross, whereat the length of each arm of the cross has to be at least two studs.
- Kind: Connector

5.2.1.8 Firewall

Generally firewalls are situated between a local network and the internet. They provide a security concept for distributed systems. To do that the user decides with the help of rules which connection to the other side of the firewall can be trusted (Fig. 5.17).[11]

Construction

- Color: Yellow
- Layout: The element is built by stacking a 1×6 bridging brick on to a 1×6 brick.
- Kind: Component

[10] Tate et al. 2006.

[11] Dustdar et al. 2003.

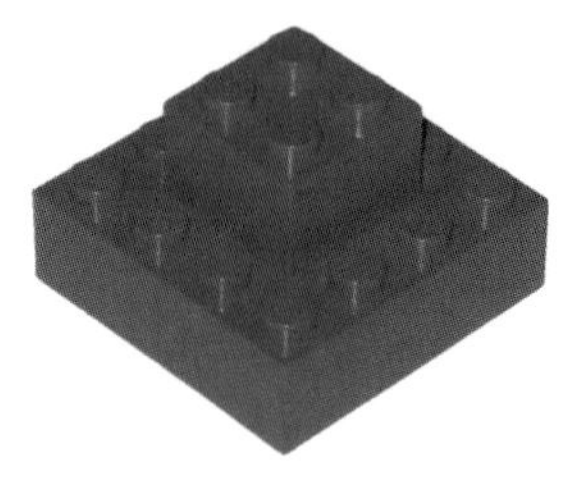

Fig. 5.18 Router

Principles of Application

The bend of the firewall's arch is indicating its strictness. A higher arch stands for a greater selection and thus for a stricter firewall.

5.2.1.9 Router

The router is a switching component within a network. It makes sure that any data traffic is forwarded to its destination (Fig. 5.18).[12]

Construction

- Color: Blue
- Layout: A router should be built like a pyramid. So use at least two 2 × 4 bricks with a 2 × 2 brick on top.
- Kind: Component

5.2.2 *Client–Server*

Elements in this group are somehow related to the client–server pattern.

5.2.2.1 Client

A client is understood to be an entity which requests and receives services. Those services are provided by any kind of server (Fig. 5.19).[13]

---

[12] Klußmann 2000.

[13] Broy and Spaniol 1999.

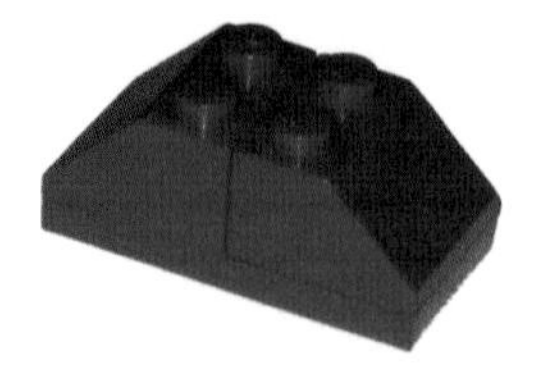

Fig. 5.19 Client

Fig. 5.20 Server

Construction

- Color: White
- Layout: Two beveled 2 × 2 bricks with the tops next to each other on one 2 × 4 plate.
- Kind: Component

Principles of Application

Clients of bigger size are of greater importance. The case study includes two clients each used to maintain the LANs. Those are built bigger than the ones which only access the LAN in a using manner. Further they are attached to the network in a more confirmative way. They contact the LAN with the whole bottom of the client-construction whereas the other clients are arranged normal to the LAN's construction and thus only contact the LAN with a subarea at their bottom.

5.2.2.2 Server

A server is a unit providing a special service. Those services which are used by clients can be of any kind (Fig. 5.20).[14]

Construction

- Color: Black
- Layout: One 2 × 4 plate on two beveled 2 × 2 bricks with the tops next to each other.
- Kind: Component

[14] Klußmann 2000.

Principles of Application

The size of the server indicates its meaning. In the case study the bigger servers represent the application servers needed for the system. The smaller ones represent servers which are only used by the system. However, they are not defined by it.

5.2.2.3 Bridge

The bridge-element is part of the Broker pattern in software architecture. Its task is to guarantee the opportunity for a broker-element to inter-operate with another broker-element (Fig. 5.21).[15]

Construction

- Color: Black
- Layout: The element is built by stacking a 1 × 6 bridging brick on to a 1 × 6 plate.
- Kind: Component

5.2.2.4 Broker

In Lévy[16] a broker-element is described to be: "... a messenger that decouples clients and servers, registers and locates servers, locates clients, forwards requests to servers, transmits results and exceptions back to clients. Moreover, it offers an API (...) to clients and servers that include operations for registering servers and for invoking server methods (Fig. 5.22)."

Fig. 5.21 Bridge

Fig. 5.22 Broker

[15] Lévy et al. 1998, p. 2.
[16] Lévy et al. 1998, p. 2.

Construction

- Color: Black
- Layout: Two beveled 2 × 2 bricks with the tops next to each other on one 2 × 4 plate on another two beveled 2 × 2 bricks with the tops next to each other.
- Kind: Component

5.2.2.5 Dispatcher

The dispatcher-element is part of the Client-Dispatcher-Server pattern. It dissolves the direct connection of client and server to hide the details about the connection from client and server and add a locally transparency (Fig. 5.23).[17]

Construction

- Color: White
- Layout: Two beveled 2 × 2 bricks with the tops next to each other on one 2 × 4 plate on another two beveled 2 × 2 bricks with the tops next to each other.
- Kind: Component

5.2.2.6 Load Balancer

Wikipedia defines a load balancer the following way (Fig. 5.24):

> ...load balancing is a technique (usually performed by load balancers) to spread work between many computers, processes, hard disks or other resources in order to get optimal resource utilization and decrease computing time.[18]

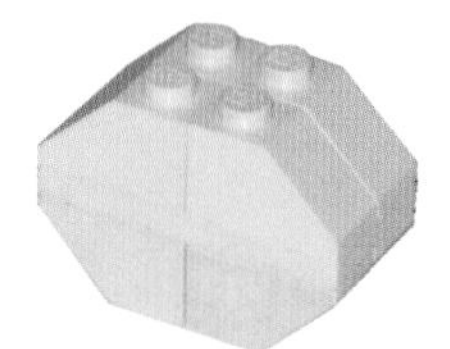

Fig. 5.23 Dispatcher

Fig. 5.24 Load balancer

[17] Dustdar et al. 2003, S. 100.

[18] Wikipedia 2007.

Construction

- Color: Red
- Layout: Two 2 × 4 bricks are placed parallel but shifted next to each other. To connect them another 2 × 4 brick is used which is stuck to both of them.
- Kind: Component

Principles of Application

Because there is only one load balancer integrated to the system of the case study there are no explicit variations.

5.2.3 Publisher–Subscriber

Elements in this group are related to the publisher–subscriber pattern.

5.2.3.1 Publisher

The publisher-element is part of the Publisher–Subscriber pattern. It is likely that the status of the publisher changes. To inform the dependent components of the software it provides notifications about its changes (Fig. 5.25).[19]

Construction

- Color: Yellow
- Layout: Two beveled 2 × 2 bricks with the highest sides next to each other on one 2 × 4 plate on another two beveled 2 × 2 bricks with the highest sides next to each other.
- Kind: Component

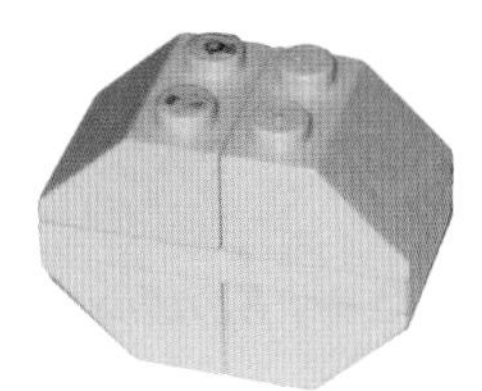

Fig. 5.25 Publisher

[18] Wikipedia 2007.

[19] Dustdar et al. 2003, S. 103.

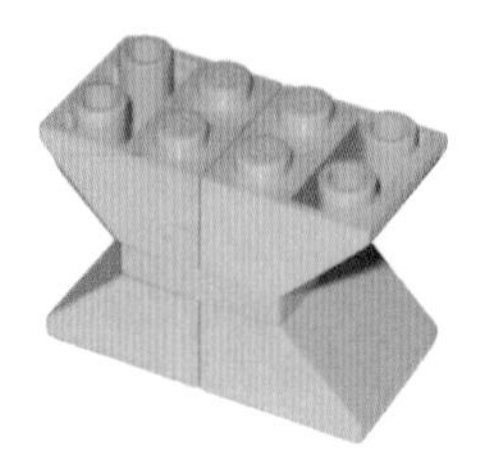

Fig. 5.26 Subscriber

Principles of Application

There is only one publisher integrated into the system of the case study. Therefore no noteworthy variation is occurs.

5.2.3.2 Subscriber

The subscriber-element is part of the Publisher–Subscriber pattern. The subscriber components of software need to be informed about changes in the publisher component. Therefore they register at the publisher to get notified in case of changes (Fig. 5.26).[20]

Construction

- Color: Yellow
- Layout: Two beveled 2×2 bricks with the highest sides next to each other on one 2×2 plate on another two beveled 2×2 bricks with the highest sides next to each other so that the shape is a cross.
- Kind: Component

Principles of Application

There is only one subscriber integrated into the system of the case study. Therefore no noteworthy variation occurs.

5.2.4 Sender–Receiver

Elements in this group are somehow related to the sender–receiver pattern.

[20] Dustdar et al. 2003, S. 103.

5.2.4.1 Sender

The sender-element is part of communication oriented architectures. It provides canals through which it sends information to prior subscribed receivers (Fig. 5.27).[21]

Construction

- Color: Blue
- Layout: Two beveled 2 × 2 bricks with the highest sides next to each other on one 2 × 4 plate on another two beveled 2 × 2 bricks with the highest sides next to each other.
- Kind: Component

5.2.4.2 Receiver

The receiver-element is part of communication oriented architectures. It is connected through canals to at least one sender. The sender feeds information to the one end of a canal which provides this information to the other end where the receiver can receipt it (Fig. 5.28).[22]

Construction

- Color: Blue
- Layout: Two beveled 2 × 2 bricks with the tops next to each other on one 2 × 2 plate on another two beveled 2 × 2 bricks with the tops next to each other so the result is cross-shaped.
- Kind: Component

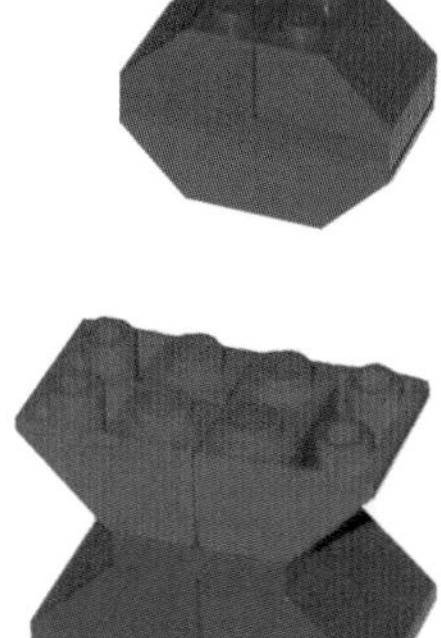

Fig. 5.27 Sender

Fig. 5.28 Receiver

[21] Dustdar et al. 2003, S. 234.
[22] Dustdar et al. 2003, S. 234.

5.2.4.3 Repeater

The repeater-element is part of communication oriented architectures in which it is primarily responsible for the scaling of the system. Repeaters receive information from senders or other repeaters to spread it out to other repeaters or receivers (Fig. 5.29).[23]

Construction

- Color: Blue
- Layout: Four 1 × 2 beveled bricks are combined with the highest side to each other so that from above the shape is a “X”. At least one 2 × 4 plate is used as bonding element.
- Kind: Component

5.2.4.4 Cache

The cache-element can be part of communication oriented architectures in which a receiver loads its contents whenever it wants to.[24] More generally it works like a buffer (Fig. 5.30).[25]

Fig. 5.29 Repeater

Fig. 5.30 Cache

[23] Dustdar et al. 2003, S. 232.
[24] Dustdar et al. 2003, S. 235.
[25] Klußmann 2000.

Construction

- Color: Blue
- Layout: Build a construction shaped like a cross with the height of two bricks.
- Kind: Component

5.2.4.5 Canal

Canals find their use in communication oriented architectures in which they connect information providers to information consumers. Those processors utilize canals to send or respectively receive information (Fig. 5.31).[26]

Construction

- Color: Green
- Layout: 2 × N plates to combine existing elements
- Kind: Connector

5.2.5 Master–Slaver

Elements in this group are related to the slave-master pattern.

5.2.5.1 Master

The master-element is part of the Master–Slave pattern. It divides the main computation into several smaller tasks which it imposes on an adequate amount of slaves so that it then can gather their achievements to combine them to the main result (Fig. 5.32).[27]

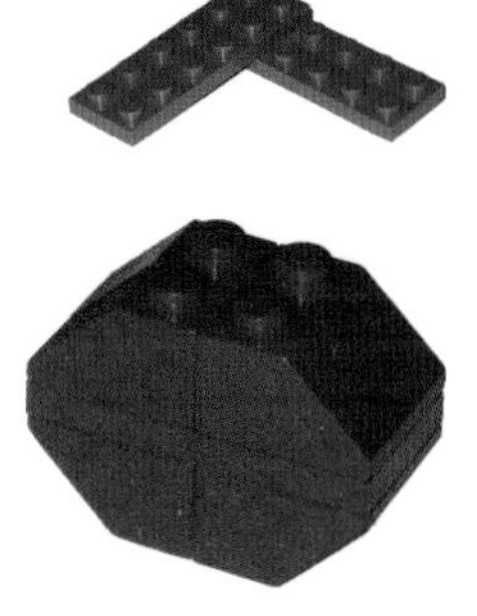

Fig. 5.31 Canal

Fig. 5.32 Master

[26] Dustdar et al. 2003, S. 232.

[27] Dustdar et al. 2003, S. 97.

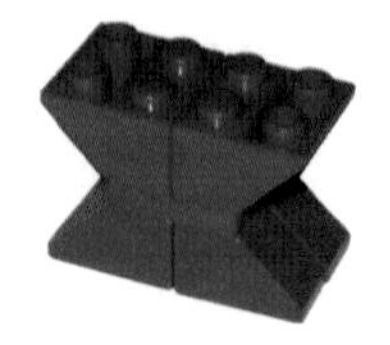

Fig. 5.33 Slave

Construction

- Color: Red
- Layout: Two beveled 2 × 2 bricks with the highest sides next to each other on one 2 × 4 plate on another two beveled 2 × 2 bricks with the highest sides next to each other.
- Kind: Component

5.2.5.2 Slave

The slave-element is part of the Master–Slave pattern. It receives tasks from the master which it computes to return the result back to its master (Fig. 5.33).[28]

Construction

- Color: Red
- Layout: Two beveled 2 × 2 bricks with the highest sides next to each other on one 2 × 2 plate on another two beveled 2 × 2 bricks with the highest sides next to each other so that the shape is a cross.
- Kind: Component

5.2.6 Pipe–Filter

Elements in this group are related to the pipe–filter pattern.

5.2.6.1 Pipe

Pipes are the transporting part of the Pipe and Filter pattern. They provide data to various filters so that they can compute it and return it back to a pipe. This results in a dataflow which is processed in an array of transformations done by the filter- and advanced by the pipe-elements (Fig. 5.34).[29]

[28] Dustdar et al. 2003, S. 97.

[29] Dustdar et al. 2003, S. 77.

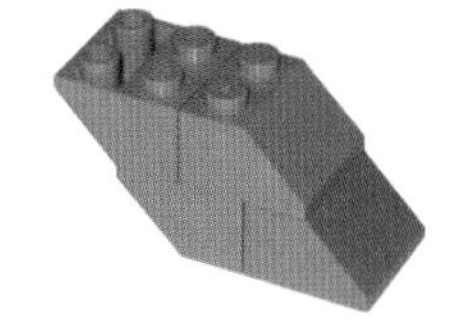

Fig. 5.34 Pipe

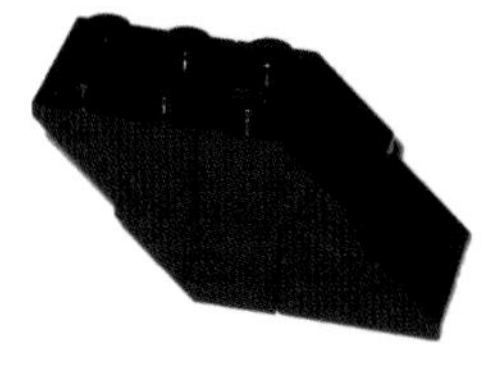

Fig. 5.35 Filter

Construction

- Color: Grey
- Layout: Two beveled 2 × 2 bricks with the highest sides next to each other on another two beveled 2 × 2 bricks with the highest sides next to each other so that the shape is skewed.
- Kind: Connector

5.2.6.2 Filter

Filters are the computing part of the Pipe and Filter pattern. They receive data from a pipe which they transform and manipulate through local rules of transformation so that they can return it back to a pipe (Fig. 5.35).[30,31]

Construction

- Color: Black
- Layout: Two beveled 2 × 2 bricks with the highest sides next to each other on another two beveled 2 × 2 bricks with the highest sides next to each other so that the shape is skewed.
- Kind: Component

[30] Dustdar et al. 2003, S. 77.

[31] Birkhölzer and Vaupel 2003, S. 87.

5.2.7 Database

Elements in this group are somehow related to the database pattern.

5.2.7.1 Database

As described in Broy[32] databases are "structured collections of persistent data which represents information." The explicit illustration of its database management system (DBMS) is not required (Fig. 5.36).

Construction

- Color: Yellow
- Layout: Databases should be shaped like the letter "L". In that manner there is a need for at least one brick on top of another whereby the one beneath is longer than the one on top. Both bricks must have the width and length of at least two studs.
- Kind: Component

Principles of Application

There is only one database integrated into the system of the case study. Therefore no noteworthy variation is occurred.

5.2.7.2 Database Management System (DBMS)

DBMS-elements provide access to data and information stored on a database. This element is only required when there is an explicit illustration of the DBMS of a database needed (Fig. 5.37).[33]

Fig. 5.36 Database

[32] Broy and Spaniol 1999.

[33] Broy and Spaniol 1999.

Construction

- Color: Green
- Layout: N × M plates to combine existing elements
- Kind: Connector

5.2.8 *Model-View-Controller*

Elements in this group are related to the model-view-controller pattern.

5.2.8.1 Model

The model-element is part of the Model-View-Controller (MVC) pattern. It is responsible for the main functionality and the data management (Fig. 5.38).[34]

Construction

- Color: Black
- Layout: Models are composed by two plates at least 4 × 4 of size which are used as ground and top respectively and at least two times two 1 × 4-bricks stacked as the sides of the entity.
- Kind: Component

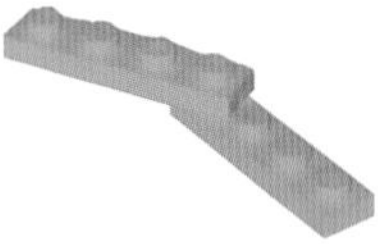

Fig. 5.37 DBMS

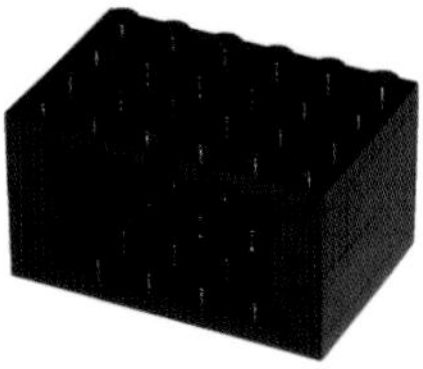

Fig. 5.38 Model

[34] Dustdar et al. 2003, S. 105.

5.2.8.2 View

The view-element is part of the Model-View-Controller (MVC) pattern. It is responsible for providing the information to the user (Fig. 5.39).[35]

Construction

- Color: Red
- Layout: Views are composed by two plates at least 4 × 4 of size which are used as ground and top respectively and at least two times two 1 × 4-bricks stacked as the sides of the entity.
- Kind: Component

5.2.8.3 Controller

The controller-element is part of the Model-View-Controller (MVC) pattern. It is responsible to compute the user inputs, controlling-, and coordination-procedures (Fig. 5.40).[36,37]

Construction

- Color: White
- Layout: Controllers are composed by two plates at least 4 × 4 of size which are used as ground and top respectively and at least two times two 1 × 4-bricks stacked as the sides of the entity.
- Kind: Component

Fig. 5.39 View

Fig. 5.40 Controller

[35] Dustdar et al. 2003, S. 105.

[36] Dustdar et al. 2003, S. 105.

[37] Birkhölzer and Vaupel 2003, S. 85.

5.2.9 Protocols

Protocols are always built with the help of Lego-plates. When they are used to only visualize the interface to another element (like JDBC to a database) it's sufficient to place an appropriate plate on to the element to illustrate that interface. But when the goal is to connect elements through a protocol (like HTTP in a network) 1 × N plates should be used to combine them. Therefore it is allowed to stack them but not to use bricks or plates with different color.

5.2.9.1 File Transfer Protocol (FTP)

The Network Working Group specifies the goals of FTP as follows (Fig. 5.41):

> The objectives of FTP are (1) to promote sharing of files (. . .), (2) to encourage indirect or implicit (. . .) use of remote computers, (3) to shield a user from variations in file storage systems among hosts, and (4) to transfer data reliably and efficiently.[38]

Construction

- Color: Blue
- Layout: N × M plates to combine existing elements
- Kind: Connector

5.2.9.2 Hypertext Transfer Protocol (HTTP)

In RFC2616 of the Network Working Group HTTP is described as "*an application-level protocol for distributed, collaborative, hypermedia information systems* (Fig. 5.42)."[39]

Fig. 5.41 FTP

Fig. 5.42 HTTP

---

[38] Postel and Reynolds (1985), p. 1.

[39] Fielding et al. 1999, p. 7.

Construction

- Color: Red
- Layout N × M plates to combine existing elements
- Kind: Connector

5.2.9.3 Java Database Connectivity (JDBC)

JDBC provides a standard to connect programs which are created with the help of the programming language Java to a wide range of databases (Fig. 5.43).[40]

Construction

- Color: White
- Layout: N × M plates to combine existing elements
- Kind: Connector

5.2.9.4 Simple Mail Transfer Protocol (SMTP)

As specified in Klensin[41] "*the objective of (...) SMTP is to transfer mail reliably and efficiently.*" And its characteristic is to be "*independent of the particular transmission subsystem*" *and to* "*require only a reliable ordered data stream channel* (Fig. 5.44)."

Construction

- Color: White
- Layout: N × M plates to combine existing elements
- Kind: Connector

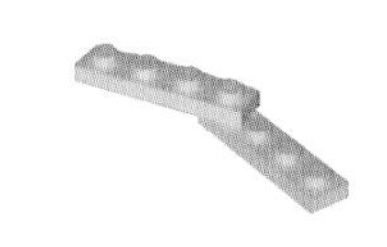

Fig. 5.43 JDBC

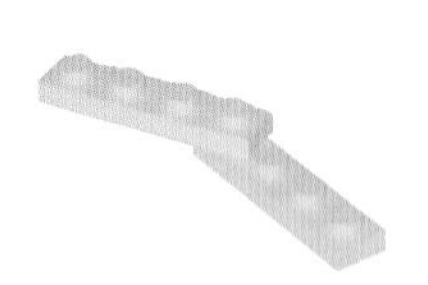

Fig. 5.44 SMTP

[40] Sun Developer Network.

[41] Klensin 2001, p. 4.

5.2.9.5 Simple Object Access Protocol (SOAP)

In Gudgin[42] SOAP is described as "*a lightweight protocol intended for exchanging structured information in a decentralized, distributed environment* (Fig. 5.45)."

Construction

- Color: Pink
- Layout: N × M plates to combine existing elements
- Kind: Connector

5.2.9.6 Transmission Control Protocol (TCP)

RFC793 specifies TCP as followed (Fig. 5.46):

> The Transmission Control Protocol (TCP) is intended for use as a highly reliable host-to-host protocol between hosts in packet-switched computer communication networks, and in interconnected systems of such networks.[43]

Construction

- Color: Black
- Layout: N × M plates to combine existing elements
- Kind: Connector

Fig. 5.45 SOAP

Fig. 5.46 TCP

[42] Gudgin et al. 2003.
[43] Information Science Institute, University of Southern California, 1981.

5.2.9.7 User Datagram Protocol (UDP)

UDP, as defined in Postel,[44] "is defined to make available a datagram mode of packed-switched computer communication in the environment of an interconnected set of computer networks. (...) This protocol provides a procedure for application programs to send messages to other programs with a minimum of protocol mechanism (Fig. 5.47)."

Construction

- Color: Grey
- Layout: N × M plates to combine existing elements
- Kind: Connector

5.2.9.8 Extensible Markup Language (XML)

As defined in Bray[45] XML "describes a class of data objects called XML documents and partially describes the behavior of computer *programs* which process them. (...) XML documents are made up of storage units called entities (Fig. 5.48)."

Construction

- Color: Orange
- Layout: N × M plates to combine existing elements
- Kind: Connector

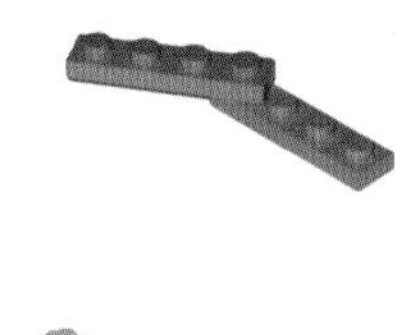

Fig. 5.47 UDP

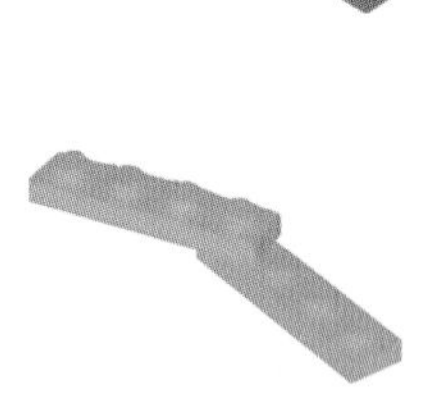

Fig. 5.48 XML

[44] Postel 1980.

[45] Bray et al. 2006.

5.2.10 *Miscellaneous*

Elements in this group are of miscellaneous nature.

5.2.10.1 Event

Events are part of event-based systems. Event-generators deliver their events to an infrastructure which provides them to interested components (Fig. 5.49).[46]

Construction

- Color: Pink
- Layout: 2 × 2 brick
- Kind: Connector

5.2.10.2 Interface Engine

The Interface Engine is part of the Interface-Engine pattern. Its field of application is to manage the data streams between independent components. For that it is translating and adjusting the interfaces or protocols of the involved components (Fig. 5.50).[47]

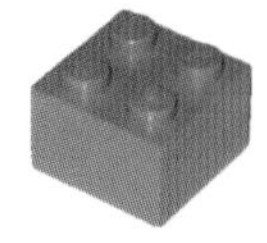

Fig. 5.49 Event

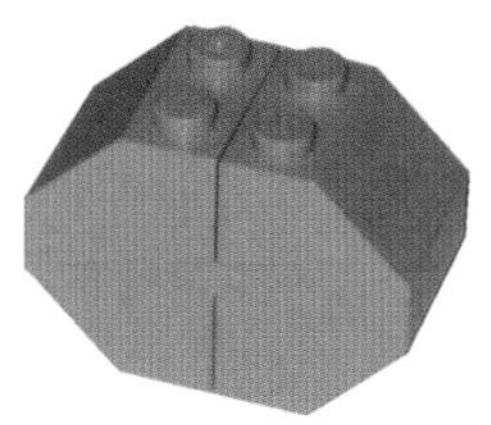

Fig. 5.50 Interface engine

[46] Dustdar et al. 2003, S. 241.

[47] Birkhölzer and Vaupel 2003, S. 83.

Construction

- Color: Grey
- Layout: Two beveled 2 × 2 bricks with the tops next to each other on one 2 × 4 plate on another two beveled 2 × 2 bricks with the tops next to each other.
- Kind: Component

5.2.10.3 Layer Borders

Layers divide software into a vertical hierarchy. They are like packages which combine parts of a software so that their services are provided to the next level of the hierarchy. On the other side contents of a layer can access the services which are provided from the lower level as well as of course the ones which are provided from the software-parts within the same layer (Fig. 5.51).[48]

Construction

- Color: Yellow
- Layout: N × M plates to distinct existing elements
- Kind: Connector

Principles of Application

Contents of one layer can only access services provided by other software of the same layer or by software contained in the underlying layer. Therefore a layer border shall always clearly single out the range of a layer.

5.2.10.4 Observer

The observer-element is part of the Observer pattern. The observing components of software need to be informed about changes in the observed component. Therefore they register at the component of interest to get notified in case of changes (Fig. 5.52).[49]

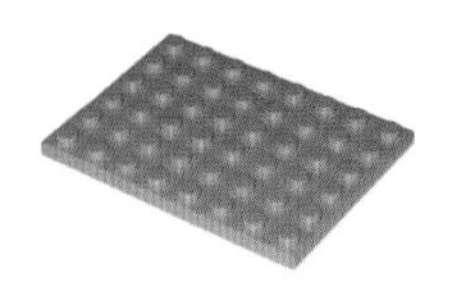

Fig. 5.51 Layer borders

---

[48] Zdun and Avgeriou 2005, p. 6.

[49] Naumovich 2002.

Construction

- Color: Blue
- Layout: Observers are composed by two plates at least 4 × 4 of size which are used as ground and top respectively and at least two times two 1 × 4-bricks stacked as the sides of the entity.
- Kind: Component

5.2.10.5 Repository

The repository-element combines equivalent components of systems to a subsystem. It provides shared interfaces to all of those systems (Fig. 5.53).[50]

Construction

- Color: Red
- Layout: Repositories should be "L"-shaped. Therefore there is a need for at least one brick on top of another whereby the one beneath is longer than the one on top. Both bricks must have the width and length of at least two studs.
- Kind: Component

Fig. 5.52 Observer

Fig. 5.53 Repository

[50] Birkhölzer and Vaupel 2003, S. 81.

5.2.10.6 Service

A service is some sort of functionality which is provided by a component so that other components can access that functionality (Fig. 5.54).[51]

Construction

- Color: Green
- Layout: 2 × 2 plates to combine existing elements.
- Kind: Connector

5.2.10.7 Datastream

The DataStream-element symbolizes like a canal the connection between two or more components. The data the stream is transporting is sequentially provided and often handled in real-time (Fig. 5.55).[52]

Construction

- Color: Blue
- Layout: 2 × N plates to combine existing elements
- Kind: Connector

5.2.11 Meta

Meta-Elements are those kind of elements which are either not important for the architecture itself but for the statics of the build Lego-construct or very special of their kind and so relevant to the current project only. They are called meta-elements

Fig. 5.54 Service

Fig. 5.55 Datastream

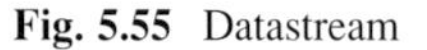

[51] Broy and Spaniol 1999.

[52] Broy and Spaniol 1999.

Fig. 5.56 Unique element

because they are only needed as placeholder for special software classes or for arrangement purposes.

5.2.11.1 Unique Elements

Unique elements are elements which are only relevant to the current project. They are too specifically to be used in other architectures. Such elements might be classes and objects deliberately designed for the software addressed by the current architecture (Fig. 5.56).

Construction

- Color: Green
- Layout: Special elements can have any kind of layout due to individual appliance
- Kind: Component

Principles of Application

Unique elements need to be applied so that their meaning for the software is not changed or lost. Appearance, layout and application of these elements are subdued to those of the other elements. In that matter they have to be adjusted in a way so that they do not disturb any other elements in their way to be built or applied.

5.2.11.2 Package

Package-elements are components, different to the ones listed above, which need an explicit annotation. They fulfill all the criteria for components (modularization, information hiding, data encapsulation, abstraction) but are too specific to allow the usage of an element above (Fig. 5.57).[53]

[53] Dustdar et al. 2003, S. 54.

Fig. 5.57 Package

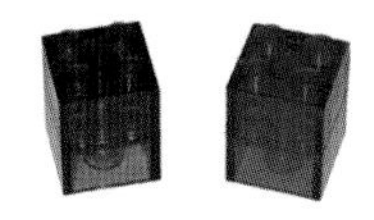

Fig. 5.58 Statics

Construction

- Color: Grey
- Layout: Packages are composed by two grey plates at least 4 $\times$ 4 of size which are used as ground and top respectively and at least two times two 1 $\times$ 4-bricks stacked as the sides of the entity.
- Kind: Component

Principles of Application

Packages symbolize a self-contained area within the software architecture. To address its contents the appropriate Lego-bricks should be placed either on top or beneath the entity depending on its wished meaning. They are especially used to realize compositions.

If the elements within a package provide defined and dedicated services to address their content all contained elements should be covered by a unique element which represents those services before the package is closed.

A package can be placed within the whole architecture so that there is no possible way to address it from outside. That means another component can only reach the content of such a package through the surrounding environment.

5.2.11.3 Lego-Statics

Lego-static-elements are only used to guarantee for the statics of the Lego-construction. The only application of these elements is to make sure that the construct does not fall apart and is compact enough so that its stability is assured (Fig. 5.58).

Construction

- Color: Transparent
- Layout: Lego-Statics can have any kind of layout
- Kind: Special, due to no transponder integration

Principles of Application

Appearance, layout and application of Lego-Statics are subdued to those of the other elements. In that matter they have to be adjusted in a way so that they do not disturb any other elements in their way to be built or applied.

Chapter 6
Case Study

This case study describes how a hypothetical example becomes an expressive and versatile guideline to generally handle a system which is meant to be implemented. The example uses Haptic System Architecture Modeling to construct the rough architecture of a system which then will be exported to Component Toolbox[1] to model the software architecture upon this system.

6.1 Introduction

6.1.1 Commercial Background

The marketing strategists of a big pharmaceutical company have perceived that direct sales of over-the-counter drugs could enable a huge price advantage over the company's competitors. By doing so the company could obtain the European market leadership within a short range of time and the production facilities could be utilized up to full capacity.

The perfect distribution channel therefore seems to be an online-shop. This strategy allows rounding out the company's incomplete product line-up with supplementing products of selected partners. In order to anticipate eventual imitators the company wants to start the online-shop simultaneously in all countries relevant for the market.

The company's IT-department does possess neither knowledge, resources nor know-how to successfully implement the aspired system. So the CTO (Chief technology officer) decides to outsource the project.

[1] Hofstetter 2007.

A. Weber and S. Dustdar, *Haptic Systems Architecture Modeling*,
DOI 10.1007/978-3-7091-0755-3_6, © Springer-Verlag/Wien 2012

Nevertheless he and his team are willing to roughly circumscribe the system's core architecture, to ensure that it is smoothly integrated into the existing IT landscape.

6.1.2 Functional Description

Customers should have the possibility to browse the product catalog using their Web- or WAP-browser (for mobile devices), to order their desired products, and to pay for them with their credit card.

Behind the scenes the orders are handled by the European central where they are processed and then forwarded to the concerning national distribution center which takes care of the actual shipping.

Assignments of the European central are:

- Providing the web shop with the own and the partners' products
- Preprocessing the orders
- Checking the credit card information
- Booking the sales (in the central accounting system)
- Forwarding the order to the national distribution center
- Using existing and collecting new customer information to provide customer specific offerings
- Forwarding of orders to the concerning distribution center

Assignments of the distribution centers are:

- Printing of delivery documents (bill, receipt, address, etc.)
- Prepackaging customers order
- Forwarding the package to the national delivery service

Due to expectations about the remarkable increased amount of orders based on the online offering, the supply chain management needs to be improved. The inventory of the national distribution centers and the European center need to be observed permanently. A purchase or delivery order is activated automatically whenever the stock falls below a certain level. To make sure the suppliers are prepared for the orders, so they on their side do not run into problems with their subcontractors, the information about the current inventory state should be made accessible to them.

So additionally to the assignments above, the European central has to provide:

- Observation of central warehouse
- Processing the orders of the national distribution centers
- Automatic order of products which stock falls under certain specific level in the central store
- Providing up-to-date information about the distribution centers' and its own inventory to the suppliers

The national distribution centers have to fulfill the following tasks:

- Observation of national storage
- Keeping the European central and the suppliers up-to-date about their inventory
- Automated ordering of products which stocks fall under their critical level

6.1.3 The Company's Approach

The IT-department of the pharmaceutical company decides to use HSAM to model the current status of the company's system due to its straightforward and uncomplicated approach.

Due to the fact that neither the company's IT-officer or his team ever used HSAM to design a system they haven't got a stock of prebuilt Lego compositions to represent specific elements. So the officer calls in the element catalogue to find out how to build up each representation for the elements they will define for the system in order to fulfill the prerequisites claimed by HSAM.

Knowing how to build the Lego compositions the IT-officer assigns most participants to construct basic representations, as shown in the first prerequisite. Simultaneously he orders a small team to prepare Lego bricks so that they are capable of holding the RFID-transponders and to integrate the tags into them, as described in the second prerequisite.

6.2 Prerequisites

At first the common prerequisites for successfully completing the HASM approach are explained. Those are, to actually build representations of the different architectural elements and the integration of the RFID transponders into those representations.

Both of the required prearrangements need to be done only once and their outcomes can be reused for later projects.

6.2.1 Building Element Representations

Each system architecture requires a set of elements integrated, combined, and interconnected to each other. In order to realize an architecture using HSAM such elements need to be represented by predefined Lego-compositions in order to be handled.

So, depending on how often a specific element is used in a system's architecture, the appropriate number of its instances needs to be built.

For the web shop system those elements are shown in the following table of illustrations. The pictures below show the smallest possible realization of an element's representation as introduced by the catalogue of element representations. Of course the actual built ones differ from those below (Figs. 6.1–6.9).

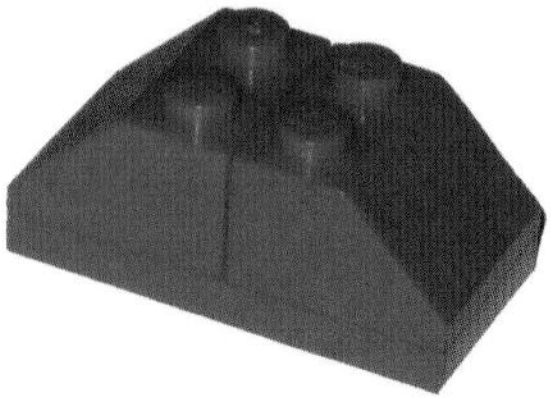

Fig. 6.1 Client

Fig. 6.2 Server

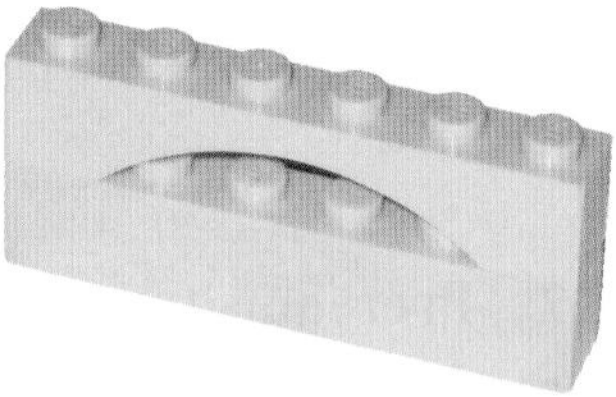

Fig. 6.3 Firewall

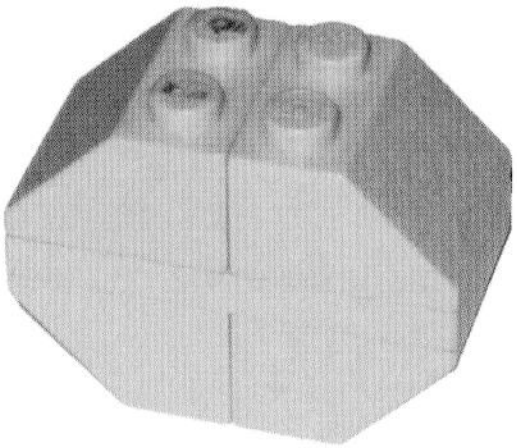

Fig. 6.4 Publisher

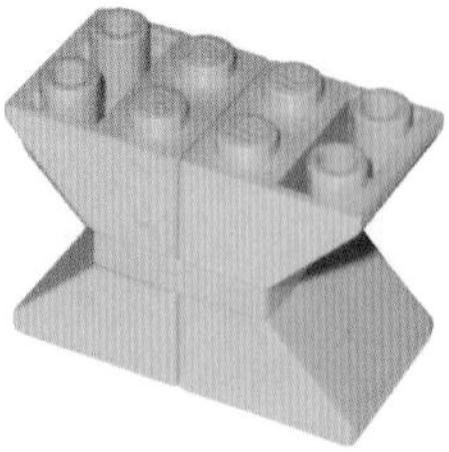

Fig. 6.5 Subscriber

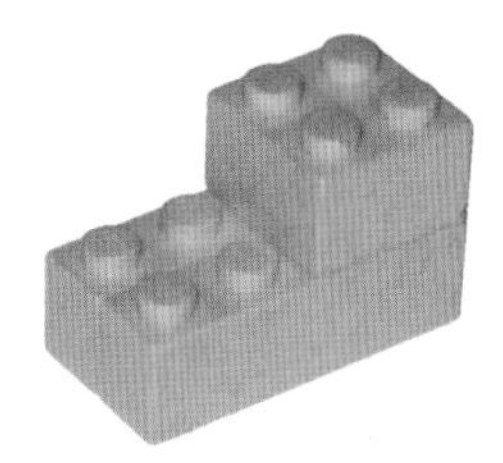

Fig. 6.6 Database

Fig. 6.7 Internet

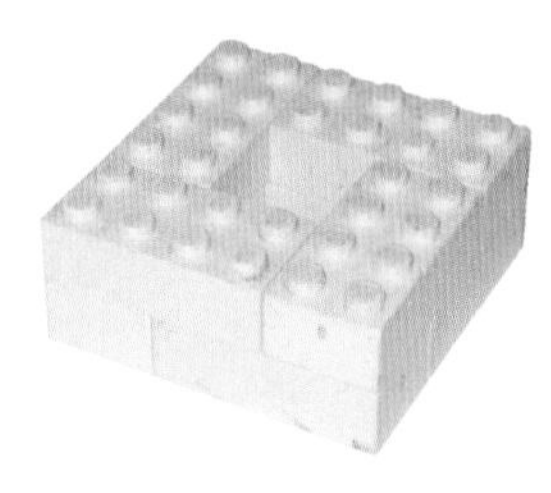

Fig. 6.8 LAN

Fig. 6.9 Intranet

6.2.2 Integrating Transponders

Integrating the RFID transponders to each element's representation is the second prerequisite to successfully execute HSAM.

In order to do so there is some customization of dedicated Lego bricks required. Orange 2×4-bricks are chosen to be those transponder-holding-bricks.

There are always two such bricks needed to hold a single RFID transponder. One of them is going to be the top of a simple construction in which both orange bricks are stuck on top of each other so that all studs of the lower brick are covered by the one above.

Consequently, in the bottom of the upper brick a slot needs to be made so that later on a transponder can be inserted. The same is required for the lower brick for which a slot is required on its top side. Then a transponder can be stuck into one of the slots so that when plugging the bricks to each other the transponder disappears into the slot of the second brick.

The following sequence of illustrations demonstrates this subject (Figs. 6.10–6.12).

When the transponders are integrated to the transponder bricks, the last necessary step is to build in those bricks into the element representations.

Due to the short range of the RFID reader, the transponder bricks need to be located at the outside of the representations. I.e. they should not be fully surrounded by the bricks used to build the representation.

However, the distinct orange bricks should be added to a Lego composition in such a way, that it is obvious that the transponder bricks belong to the representation which references to the kind of element the transponder is tagged to. I.e. as far as possible the bricks should not be able to touch any other representation than the one they are added to.

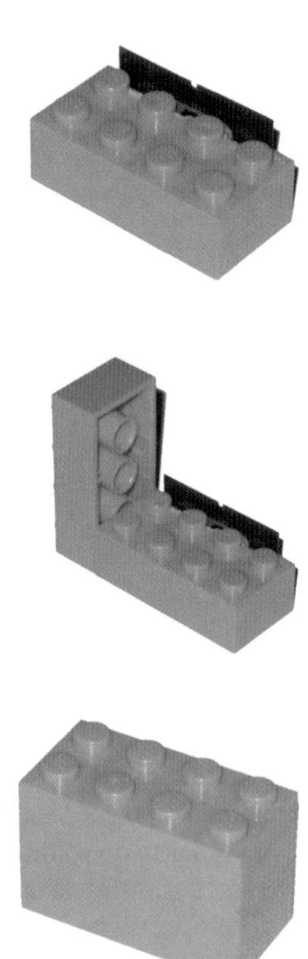

Fig. 6.10 Integrated transponder

Fig. 6.11 Transponder bricks

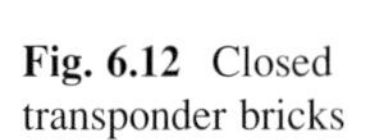

Fig. 6.12 Closed transponder bricks

If for any reason an obvious integration is not possible, e.g. for protocols, then the transponder bricks should be located in a way that at least no other representation within the architecture gets in touch with those orange bricks.

The following illustrations show the element representations holding each a transponder brick and used for the web shop system later on Figs. 6.13–6.21.

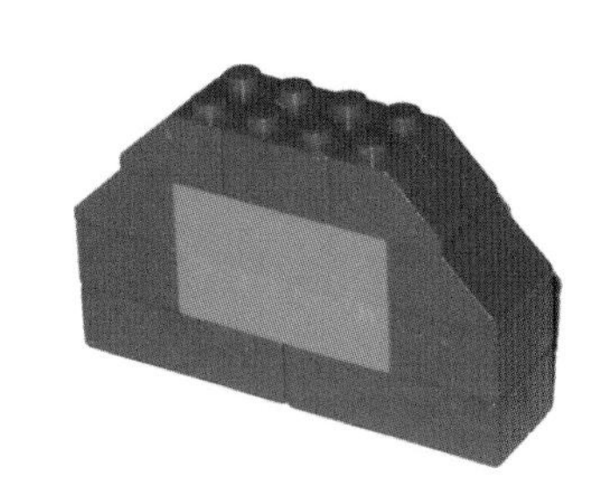

Fig. 6.13 Client with transponder bricks

Fig. 6.14 Server with transponder bricks

Fig. 6.15 Firewall with transponder bricks

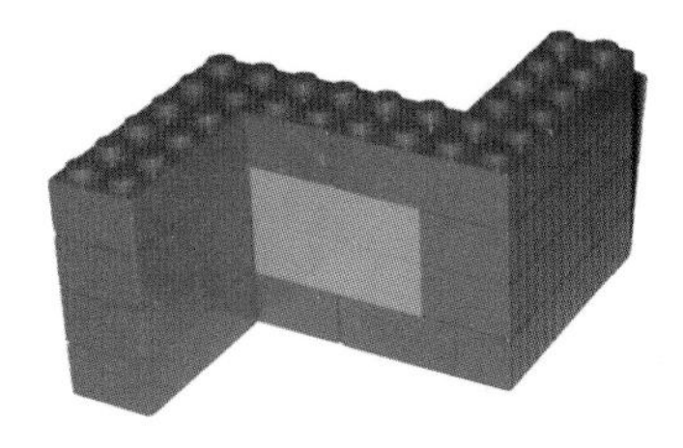

Fig. 6.16 Load balancer with transponder bricks

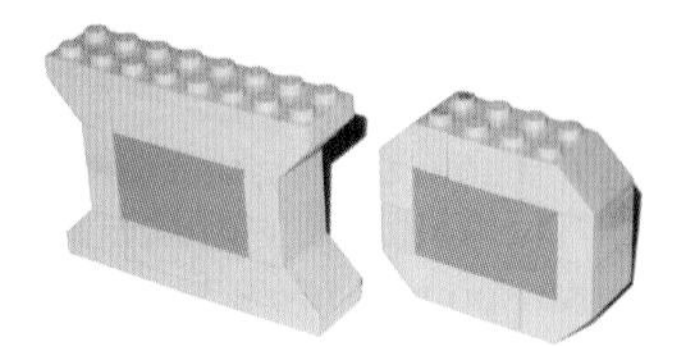

Fig. 6.17 Publisher/Subscriber with transponder bricks

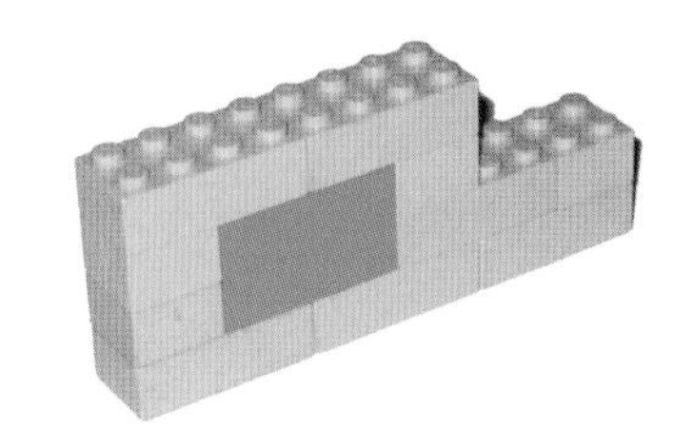

Fig. 6.18 Database with transponder bricks

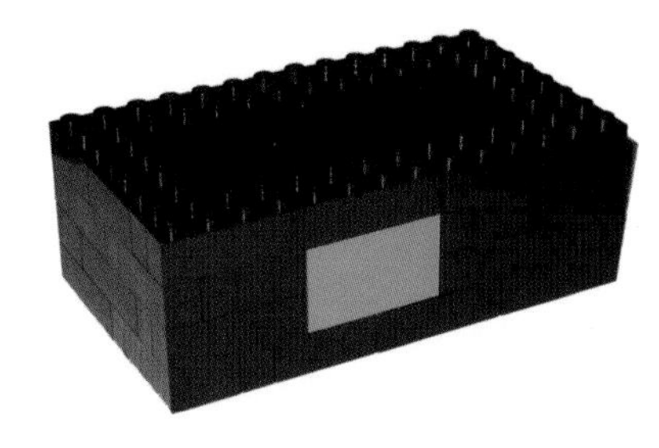

Fig. 6.19 Internet with transponder bricks

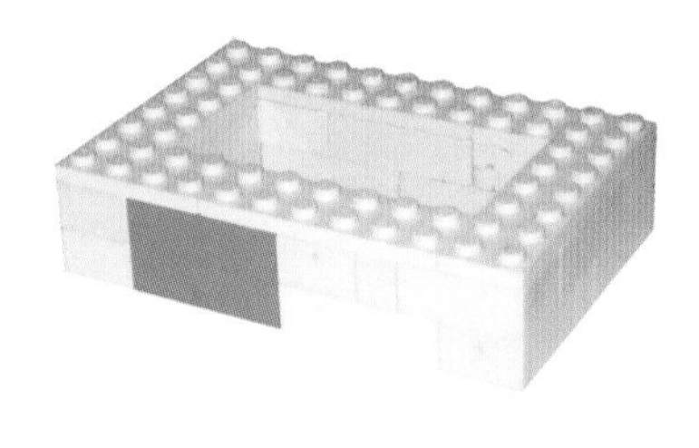

Fig. 6.20 LAN with transponder bricks

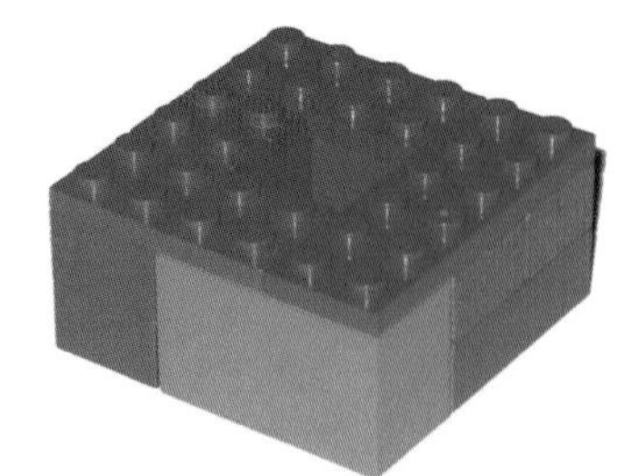

Fig. 6.21 Intranet with transponder bricks

6.3 Process HSAM

This section describes how the company's IT-officer and his team complete the recurring actions in order to correctly process HSAM. Those actions are the following:

- Find all architectural elements
- Shape those elements
- Tag those elements
- Build the architecture
- Read in the architecture
- Configure its elements
- Export the architecture

6.3.1 Architectural Elements

The IT-officer arranges a meeting with specialists from the sub-departments to conduct the process specified by this new approach.

Together they gather around a table to, first, brainstorm for elements which are in use for the current system. For that, some of the coworkers brought files which contain detailed information about parts of the system, like the configurations of the workstations or how the local and international networks are built up.

The IT-officer defines, as the first step for the working team to do, to find distinct elements of the system which would be relevant to a web-shop-system based on the information all the participants brought along. The following listing is the result of the analysis for each the international as well as the national network:

- International network:
  - Admin client
  - Firewall
  - Database
  - Stock-server
  - Accounting-server
  - Application-server
- National network:
  - Admin client
  - Firewall
  - Application-server

Of course they notice that the existing parts of the system which would be useful for a web shop are not sufficient. So the IT-officer orders to brainstorm for additional elements such a targeted system would require. They all agree that the following list of additional elements is required:

- Customer PC: The web-shop needs to consider possible customers, who visit the shop using a conventional browser,
- Customer mobile: The company would like to also make the shop available for mobile devices,
- Load balancer: Because of the predicted impact of the new way of sale the IT-officer wants to make sure no delay for visiting the shop should occur,
- Web-server: All the participants agree that the shop should run on dedicated servers,
- Firewall: Due to security reasons firewalls should be installed between the load balancer and the internet and between the web server and the international network,
- Publisher: The team wants to provide a publisher at the international network in order enable the company's headquarter to inform the national networks about important incidents,
- Subscriber: On the other side the national network needs a subscriber to be able to get informed through the publisher,
- Stock-server: Because the national office takes over the shipping of the articles which can be ordered through the web shop it needs to feature a warehouse. The stock server provides the system about its condition,
- Print-server: The national distribution center should be in charge to provide the accompanying papers of a purchase to the customers,
- Billing server: The team knows that another company is already providing a billing server which now should be used by the web shop system,
- Content server: An external content server seems to be handy to scale the web-shop functionality,
- Supplier server: The new system should offer suppliers the possibility to autonomous service their products. The updates for the web shop should be gotten through a provided server.

6.3.2 Shaping Elements

After double-checking the list of system elements they need for the shop system the team-leader reads through the next step of the instructions noticing that varying the shapes of the Lego composition facilitates the distinction of elements of the same kind. So he orders the element-building-group to alter the shapes of some elements to assign special attributes to them.

After combining the two team's work so that they now have variable shaped element representations with integrated transponder bricks the outcome looks like the following:

- Clients: The team identified four clients whereas the two broader ones represent the administration clients for the national and the international network. The other two are for possible customers using a browser or WAP-access.
- Servers: Multiple servers are needed to represent both external servers as well as servers defined by the new system. The broader shaped elements stand for either application servers or a web server.
- Firewalls: Because the web server should obtain an own access to the internet another two firewalls are needed. The ones which consist of a higher arch represent firewalls which are located between the internet and the system. The other one should be located between the international network and the web server.
- Database: There is need for only one database so that there was no alteration of its shape required.
- Load balancer: As for the database, only one load balancer is needed to build up the system's architecture.
- Publisher –Subscriber: Publisher and subscriber are only appearing once in the system. Nevertheless, the IT-officer wants them to be of same size.
- Internet: A single Lego composition is needed to represent the internet. But because in reality it is the biggest network the team also builds it the biggest network in the system.
- LANs: There are two representations required for LAN. The smaller ring should stand for the national and the bigger one for the international LAN.
- Intranets: Because the IT-officer learned that a component can only be connected to a connecting element they add some intranet elements to be capable of connecting the appropriate elements.

6.3.3 Tagging Elements

The IT-officer now follows the next step of the HSAM-instructions to tag each element with its appropriate type using the HSAM-Tool. To do so, he previously told the proper department of the company to purchase the same RFID-reader as used in the instructions to guarantee its successful execution as well as installed the tool as mentioned in the user guide.

In order to successfully tag each Lego composition the IT-officer first needs to connect the reader to the HSAM-Tool. As he had found out earlier the reader will be connected through COM-port 3. So he selects the appropriate port in the list and establishes the connection to it.

After the tool has detected the RFID-reader and created the connection, it provides some information to the user so that the reader can be identified as the one which is needed for the tagging process.

When the reader is connected to the HSAM-Tool the IT-officer opens the dialogue to tag each element. He takes one element representation after each

Fig. 6.22 Tag element with reader

other to place it right in front of the reader (see Fig. 6.22), chooses the right kind of element in the list of the tagging dialogue, and hits the appropriate button so that the tool references the tag-id to the selected kind of element.

He repeats this step for each of the elements he and his team have decided to add to the web shop system.

After the references from all representations to their appropriate kind of element are established the IT-officer disconnects the RFID reader from the tool as it will not be needed anymore for some time.

6.3.4 Building the Architecture

Now that all is set to construct the architecture using the Lego compositions, the team tries different ways to attach the elements to each other interchanging ideas and thoughts about the possible outcomes until they have the same opinion about the correctness of their construction.

The following illustrations show some intermediate results, an attempts for the whole architecture, and, at last, the resulting Lego-construction of their work.

Figure 6.23 shows an example of the whole architecture but some of the team members wanted to discard this result because they had concerns about the security of the whole system. They insisted on adding firewalls between the internet and the load balancer and between the international LAN and the web server. Furthermore, they thought that an extra connection between the international LAN and the internet would be advantageous. The team members wanted to provide a direct connection to the internet for the application server within the international LAN.

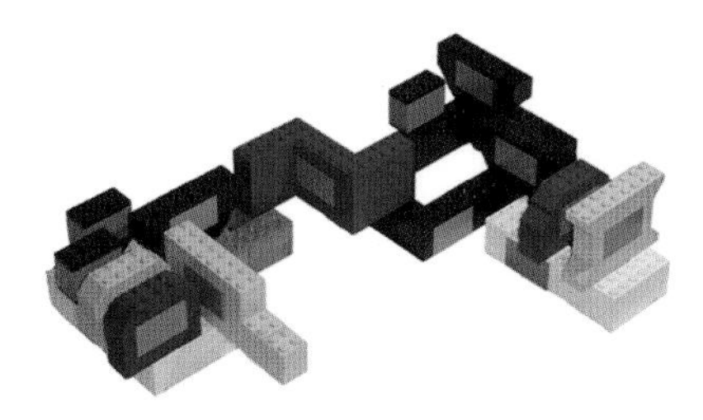

Fig. 6.23 Wrong approach to desired system architecture

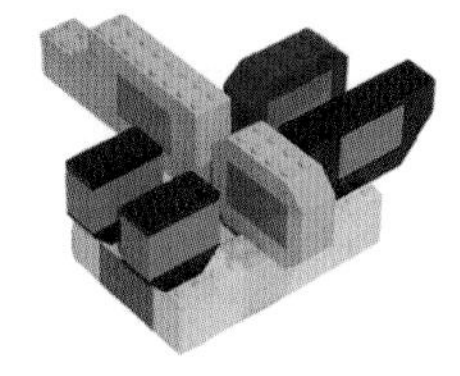

Fig. 6.24 Intermediate result – international LAN

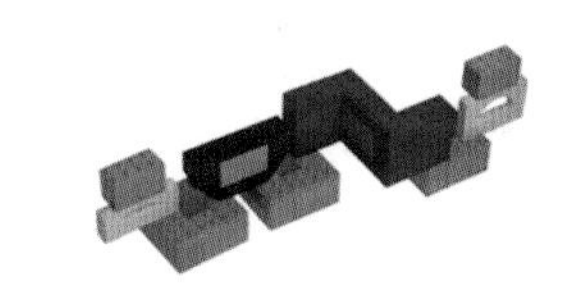

Fig. 6.25 Intermediate result – web server connection

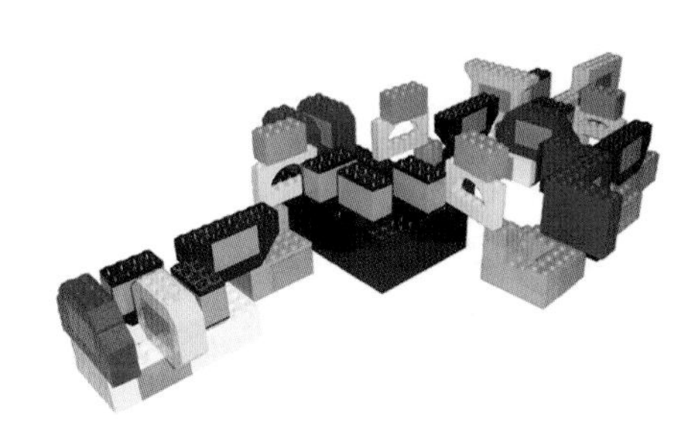

Fig. 6.26 The resulting web shop system built with HSAM

Figure 6.24 shows the intermediate result for the international LAN. It already connects all the relevant components but still misses the connections to the other parts of the architecture, like the internet or the web server.

Figure 6.25 illustrates the structure for the web server. It provides a firewall on both ends to be connected to the international LAN as well as the internet. The web server and the load balancer are connected through intranet elements.

However, Fig. 6.26 shows the result of the web shop's system architecture the IT-officer and all his team members are satisfied with.

After the successful construction of the company's current system architecture the IT-officer supervises the validation process of the system done by his team. Because the working group already performed validation tests during the construction process, as can be seen comparing Figs. 6.24 and 6.25 to Fig. 6.23, no alterations of the Lego building are needed so that the final test is only necessary for a final check.

6.3.5 Read in the Architecture

Now that the construction part of HSAM is done the IT-officer uses the HSAM-Tool to, once again, connect the RFID reader to the HSAM-Tool. Then he opens the appropriate dialogue to read in each element.

To do so the IT-officer places the reader in front of each element so that the head of the reader points directly to the transponder bricks of the representation (see Fig. 6.27).

He performs the read in process in the following sequence: First the IT-officer reads in a connecting element to then read in all the components it is connecting. He consequently repeats this step for each connector in order to already establish the right connections between components and connectors as he reads in the architecture.

The read in process opens the opportunity to configure an element while it's still obvious what element just was handled. Because there is no possibility for the tool to identify the exact values for the properties of an element, it adds default values to the read in ones, which in turn makes it harder for the team to provide the proper values to the appropriate properties in case of configuration after the whole read in process.

6.3.6 Configuring the Elements

So the IT-officer decides that after each successful read in the element should be provided with the appropriate values for its properties based on the numerous papers the participants brought along.

By double-clicking on an element listed in the HSAM-Tool on the left side (see Fig. 6.28) he reaches the element's details (see Fig. 6.29). With the help of the

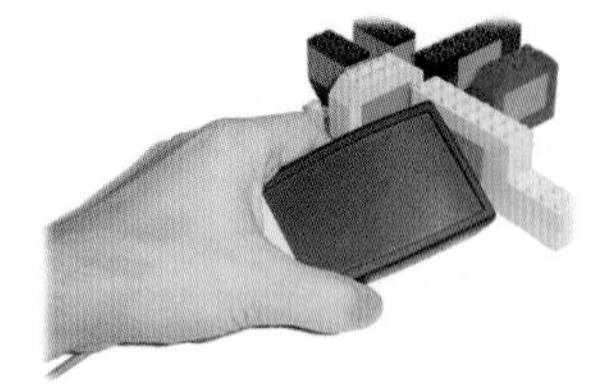

Fig. 6.27 Read in an element of the architecture

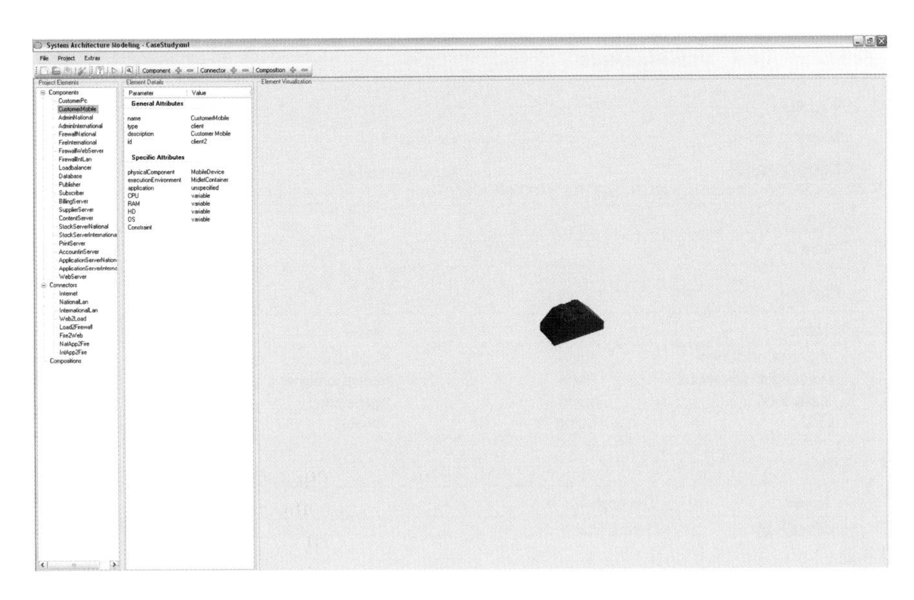

Fig. 6.28 Read in architecture

appearing dialogue he can configure all attributes and properties provided as default by the HSAM-Tool as well as add additional information as properties to the element.

More attention is to turn to the default properties provided by the program for each element relevant to export the project to Component Toolbox. Some properties which are provided by the HSAM-Tool define fundamental attributes for the system in Component Toolbox. Those attributes are now matter of interest for the workgroup. Through them the team around the IT-officer defines at what stage of implementation each element needs to be realized.

Those stages of implementation are the physical component itself, the execution environment and the kind of application. Physical component defines in what physical way the component is realized in the real world. Execution environment specifies the kind of operating system the following applications are based on. And application defines what kind of application corresponds to the component.

So for each component the team chooses its physical character as value of the parameter *physical component*. E.g. for servers which only provide services for the web shop but cannot be affected by the system, like the supplier-server, they define *externalSystem* for its value.

As the team can configure the physical component they can choose the character for the execution environment and the application.

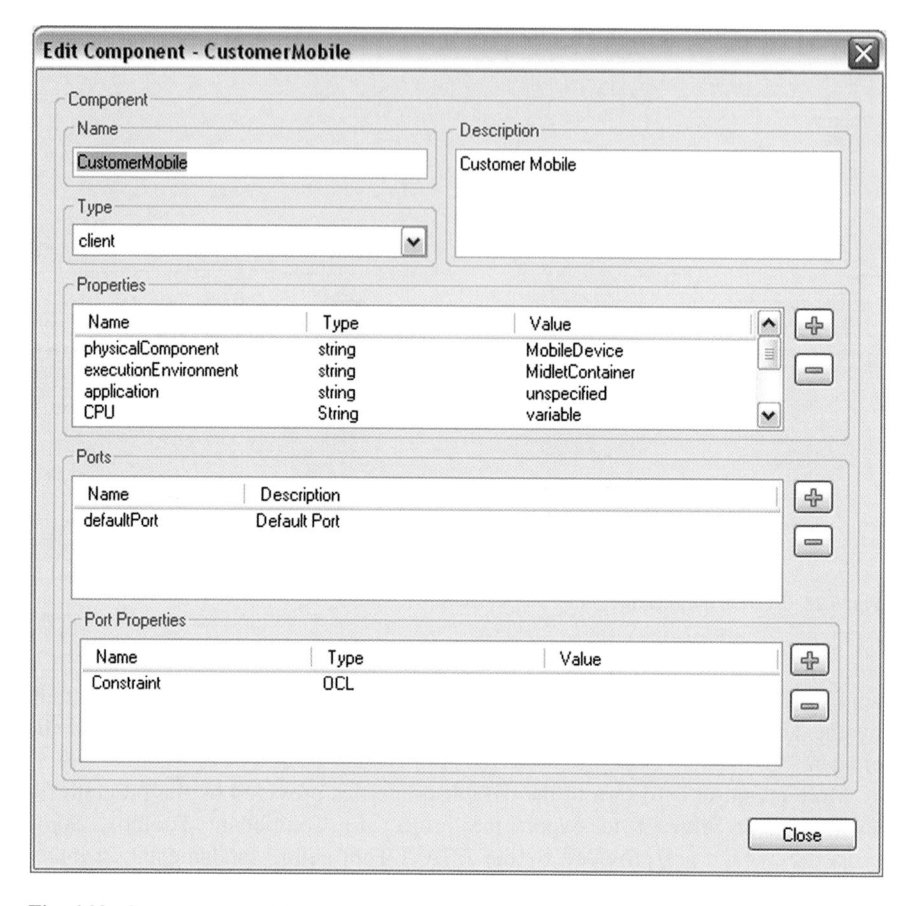

Fig. 6.29 Component's details

Of course the team specifies more parameters and their values for each element based on the information they extract out of their documents. All the entered values can be seen in the project xml provided by the next step.

6.3.7 *Exporting the Architecture*

The actual building and handling part of the HSAM approach is now done. The IT-officer has to decide how to proceed with the architecture from now on.

At first he saves the project which now consists of all elements they have read in plus their specifications they have extracted out of their papers. He orders a team member to file it for archive purposes. The saved project looks like the following:

```
<?xml version="1.0" encoding="ISO-8859-1"?>
<Project xml-version="1.0" name="CaseStudy" author="IT-officer"
  date="16.09.2007 14:18:20" xmlns:xsi="http://www.w3.org/2001/XMLSchema-
  instance" xsi:noNamespaceSchemaLocation="HSAM.xsd">
  <Properties>
    <Property name="Constraint" type="OCL" value="" meta="invisible" />
  </Properties>
  <Components>
    <Component name="CustomerPc" type="client" description="Customer PC"
      id="client1">
      <Properties>
        <Property name="physicalComponent" type="string" value="WorkStation"
          meta="visible" />
        <Property name="executionEnvironment" type="string"
          value="GenericContainer" meta="visible" />
        <Property name="application" type="string" value="unspecified"
          meta="invisible" />
        <Property name="CPU" type="String" value="variable" meta="invisible"/>
        <Property name="RAM" type="String" value="variable" meta="invisible"/>
        <Property name="HD" type="String" value="variable" meta="invisible" />
        <Property name="OS" type="String" value="variable" meta="invisible" />
        <Property name="Constraint" type="OCL" value="" meta="invisible" />
      </Properties>
      <Ports>
        <Port name="defaultPort" description="Default Port"
          id="client1_port1">
          <Properties>
            <Property name="Constraint" type="OCL" value="" meta="" />
          </Properties>
        </Port>
      </Ports>
    </Component>
    <Component name="CustomerMobile" type="client" description="Customer
      Mobile" id="client2">
      <Properties>
        <Property name="physicalComponent" type="string" value="MobileDevice"
          meta="visible" />
        <Property name="executionEnvironment" type="string"
          value="MidletContainer" meta="visible" />
        <Property name="application" type="string" value="unspecified"
          meta="invisible" />
        <Property name="CPU" type="String" value="variable" meta="invisible"/>
        <Property name="RAM" type="String" value="variable" meta="invisible"/>
        <Property name="HD" type="String" value="variable" meta="invisible" />
        <Property name="OS" type="String" value="variable" meta="invisible" />
        <Property name="Constraint" type="OCL" value="" meta="invisible" />
      </Properties>
      <Ports>
        <Port name="defaultPort" description="Default Port"
          id="client2_port1">
          <Properties>
            <Property name="Constraint" type="OCL" value="" meta="" />
          </Properties>
        </Port>
      </Ports>
    </Component>
```

```
<Component name="AdminNational" type="client" description="National Admin"
  id="client3">
  <Properties>
    <Property name="physicalComponent" type="string" value="WorkStation"
      meta="visible" />
    <Property name="executionEnvironment" type="string"
      value="GenericContainer" meta="visible" />
    <Property name="application" type="string" value="unspecified"
      meta="invisible" />
    <Property name="CPU" type="Integer" value="2400" meta="visible" />
    <Property name="RAM" type="Integer" value="2048" meta="visible" />
    <Property name="HD" type="Integer" value="80" meta="visible" />
    <Property name="OS" type="String" value="WinXP" meta="visible" />
    <Property name="Constraint" type="OCL" value="" meta="invisible" />
  </Properties>
  <Ports>
    <Port name="defaultPort" description="Default Port"
      id="client3_port1">
      <Properties>
        <Property name="Constraint" type="OCL" value="" meta="" />
      </Properties>
    </Port>
  </Ports>
</Component>
<Component name="AdminInternational" type="client"
  description="International Client" id="client4">
  <Properties>
    <Property name="physicalComponent" type="string" value="WorkStation"
      meta="visible" />
    <Property name="executionEnvironment" type="string"
      value="GenericContainer" meta="visible" />
    <Property name="application" type="string" value="unspecified"
      meta="invisible" />
    <Property name="CPU" type="Integer" value="2400" meta="visible" />
    <Property name="RAM" type="Integer" value="2048" meta="visible" />
    <Property name="HD" type="Integer" value="80" meta="visible" />
    <Property name="OS" type="String" value="WinXP" meta="visible" />
    <Property name="Constraint" type="OCL" value="" meta="invisible" />
  </Properties>
  <Ports>
    <Port name="defaultPort" description="Default Port"
      id="client4_port1">
      <Properties>
        <Property name="Constraint" type="OCL" value="" meta="" />
      </Properties>
    </Port>
  </Ports>
</Component>
<Component name="FirewallNational" type="firewall" description="National
  Firewall" id="firewall1">
  <Properties>
    <Property name="physicalComponent" type="string" value="GenericDevice"
      meta="visible" />
    <Property name="executionEnvironment" type="string"
      value="GenericContainer" meta="visible" />
    <Property name="application" type="string" value="Firewall"
      meta="visible" />
    <Property name="Constraint" type="OCL" value="" meta="invisible" />
  </Properties>
  <Ports>
    <Port name="defaultPort" description="Default Port"
      id="firewall1_port1">
      <Properties>
        <Property name="Constraint" type="OCL" value="" meta="" />
      </Properties>
```

```
      </Port>
    </Ports>
  </Component>
  <Component name="FireInternational" type="firewall" description="Firewall
    for international AppServer" id="firewall2">
    <Properties>
      <Property name="physicalComponent" type="string" value="GenericDevice"
        meta="visible" />
      <Property name="executionEnvironment" type="string"
        value="GenericContainer" meta="visible" />
      <Property name="application" type="string" value="Firewall"
        meta="visible" />
      <Property name="Constraint" type="OCL" value="" meta="invisible" />
    </Properties>
    <Ports>
      <Port name="defaultPort" description="Default Port"
        id="firewall2_port1">
        <Properties>
          <Property name="Constraint" type="OCL" value="" meta="" />
        </Properties>
      </Port>
    </Ports>
  </Component>
  <Component name="FirewallWebServer" type="firewall" description="Firewall
    for WebServers" id="firewall3">
    <Properties>
      <Property name="physicalComponent" type="string" value="GenericDevice"
        meta="visible" />
      <Property name="executionEnvironment" type="string"
        value="GenericContainer" meta="visible" />
      <Property name="application" type="string" value="Firewall"
        meta="visible" />
      <Property name="Constraint" type="OCL" value="" meta="invisible" />
    </Properties>
    <Ports>
      <Port name="defaultPort" description="Default Port"
        id="firewall3_port1">
        <Properties>
          <Property name="Constraint" type="OCL" value="" meta="" />
        </Properties>
      </Port>
    </Ports>
  </Component>
  <Component name="FirewallIntLan" type="firewall" description="Firewall for
    international Lan" id="firewall4">
    <Properties>
      <Property name="physicalComponent" type="string" value="GenericDevice"
        meta="visible" />
      <Property name="executionEnvironment" type="string"
        value="GenericContainer" meta="visible" />
      <Property name="application" type="string" value="Firewall"
        meta="visible" />
      <Property name="Constraint" type="OCL" value="" meta="invisible" />
    </Properties>
    <Ports>
      <Port name="defaultPort" description="Default Port"
        id="firewall4_port1">
        <Properties>
          <Property name="Constraint" type="OCL" value="" meta="" />
        </Properties>
      </Port>
    </Ports>
  </Component>
  <Component name="Loadbalancer" type="loadbalancer"
    description="Loabbalancer for WebServers" id="loadbalancer1">
    <Properties>
      <Property name="physicalComponent" type="string" value="GenericDevice"
        meta="visible" />
```

```
    <Property name="executionEnvironment" type="string"
      value="GenericContainer" meta="visible" />
    <Property name="application" type="string" value="LoadBalancer"
      meta="visible" />
    &lt;Property name="Constraint" type="OCL" value="" meta="invisible" /&gt;
  &lt;/Properties&gt;
  &lt;Ports&gt;
    <Port name="defaultPort" description="Default Port"
      id="loadbalancer1_port1">
      &lt;Properties&gt;
        &lt;Property name="Constraint" type="OCL" value="" meta="" /&gt;
      &lt;/Properties&gt;
    &lt;/Port&gt;
  &lt;/Ports&gt;
&lt;/Component&gt;
<Component name="Database" type="database" description="Database for
  Customers &amp; Products" id="database1">
  &lt;Properties&gt;
    <Property name="physicalComponent" type="string" value="MainFrame"
      meta="visible" />
    <Property name="executionEnvironment" type="string"
      value="GenericContainer" meta="visible" />
    <Property name="application" type="string" value="Database"
      meta="visible" />
    &lt;Property name="CPU" type="Integer" value="3000" meta="visible" /&gt;
    &lt;Property name="RAM" type="Integer" value="8192" meta="visible" /&gt;
    &lt;Property name="HD" type="Integer" value="160" meta="visible" /&gt;
    &lt;Property name="OS" type="String" value="SUSE" meta="visible" /&gt;
    &lt;Property name="Constraint" type="OCL" value="" meta="invisible" /&gt;
  &lt;/Properties&gt;
  &lt;Ports&gt;
    <Port name="defaultPort" description="Default Port"
      id="database1_port1">
      &lt;Properties&gt;
        &lt;Property name="Constraint" type="OCL" value="" meta="" /&gt;
      &lt;/Properties&gt;
    &lt;/Port&gt;
  &lt;/Ports&gt;
&lt;/Component&gt;
<Component name="Publisher" type="publisher" description="Publisher in
  international Lan" id="publisher1">
  &lt;Properties&gt;
    <Property name="physicalComponent" type="string" value="MainFrame"
      meta="visible" />
    <Property name="executionEnvironment" type="string"
      value="GenericContainer" meta="visible" />
    <Property name="application" type="string" value="MessagingSystem"
      meta="visible" />
    &lt;Property name="CPU" type="Integer" value="2400" meta="visible" /&gt;
    &lt;Property name="RAM" type="Integer" value="8192" meta="visible" /&gt;
    &lt;Property name="HD" type="Integer" value="160" meta="visible" /&gt;
    &lt;Property name="OS" type="String" value="SUSE" meta="visible" /&gt;
    &lt;Property name="Constraint" type="OCL" value="" meta="invisible" /&gt;
  &lt;/Properties&gt;
  &lt;Ports&gt;
    <Port name="defaultPort" description="Default Port"
      id="publisher1_port1">
      &lt;Properties&gt;
        &lt;Property name="Constraint" type="OCL" value="" meta="" /&gt;
      &lt;/Properties&gt;
    &lt;/Port&gt;
  &lt;/Ports&gt;
&lt;/Component&gt;
<Component name="Subscriber" type="subscriber" description="Subscriber for
  national Lan" id="subscriber1">
  &lt;Properties&gt;
    <Property name="physicalComponent" type="string" value="MainFrame"
      meta="visible" />
```

```
    <Property name="executionEnvironment" type="string"
      value="GenericContainer" meta="visible" />
    <Property name="application" type="string" value="MessagingSystem"
      meta="visible" />
    <Property name="CPU" type="Integer" value="2400" meta="visible" />
    <Property name="RAM" type="Integer" value="8192" meta="visible" />
    <Property name="HD" type="Integer" value="120" meta="visible" />
    <Property name="OS" type="String" value="SUSE" meta="visible" />
    <Property name="Constraint" type="OCL" value="" meta="invisible" />
  </Properties>
  <Ports>
    <Port name="defaultPort" description="Default Port"
      id="subscriber1_port1">
      <Properties>
        <Property name="Constraint" type="OCL" value="" meta="" />
      </Properties>
    </Port>
  </Ports>
</Component>
<Component name="BillingServer" type="server" description="external
  billing server" id="server1">
  <Properties>
    <Property name="physicalComponent" type="string"
      value="ExternalSystem" meta="visible" />
    <Property name="executionEnvironment" type="string"
      value="unspecified" meta="invisible" />
    <Property name="application" type="string" value="unspecified"
      meta="invisible" />
    <Property name="CPU" type="integer" value="" meta="invisible" />
    <Property name="RAM" type="integer" value="" meta="invisible" />
    <Property name="HD" type="integer" value="" meta="invisible" />
    <Property name="OS" type="string" value="" meta="invisible" />
    <Property name="Constraint" type="OCL" value="" meta="invisible" />
  </Properties>
  <Ports>
    <Port name="defaultPort" description="Default Port"
      id="server1_port1">
      <Properties>
        <Property name="Constraint" type="OCL" value="" meta="" />
      </Properties>
    </Port>
  </Ports>
</Component>
<Component name="SupplierServer" type="server" description="external
  SupplierServer" id="server2">
  <Properties>
    <Property name="physicalComponent" type="string"
      value="ExternalSystem" meta="visible" />
    <Property name="executionEnvironment" type="string"
      value="unspecified" meta="invisible" />
    <Property name="application" type="string" value="unspecified"
      meta="invisible" />
    <Property name="CPU" type="integer" value="" meta="invisible" />
    <Property name="RAM" type="integer" value="" meta="invisible" />
    <Property name="HD" type="integer" value="" meta="invisible" />
    <Property name="OS" type="string" value="" meta="invisible" />
    <Property name="Constraint" type="OCL" value="" meta="invisible" />
  </Properties>
  <Ports>
    <Port name="defaultPort" description="Default Port"
      id="server2_port1">
      <Properties>
        <Property name="Constraint" type="OCL" value="" meta="" />
      </Properties>
    </Port>
  </Ports>
</Component>
<Component name="ContentServer" type="server" description="external
```

```
    ContentServer" id="server3">
    <Properties>
      <Property name="physicalComponent" type="string"
        value="ExternalSystem" meta="visible" />
      <Property name="executionEnvironment" type="string"
        value="unspecified" meta="invisible" />
      <Property name="application" type="string" value="unspecified"
        meta="invisible" />
      <Property name="CPU" type="integer" value="" meta="invisible" />
      <Property name="RAM" type="integer" value="" meta="invisible" />
      <Property name="HD" type="integer" value="" meta="invisible" />
      <Property name="OS" type="string" value="" meta="invisible" />
      <Property name="Constraint" type="OCL" value="" meta="invisible" />
    </Properties>
    <Ports>
      <Port name="defaultPort" description="Default Port"
        id="server3_port1">
        <Properties>
          <Property name="Constraint" type="OCL" value="" meta="" />
        </Properties>
      </Port>
    </Ports>
  </Component>
  <Component name="StockServerNational" type="server" description="external
    StockServer for national Lan" id="server4">
    <Properties>
      <Property name="physicalComponent" type="string"
        value="ExternalSystem" meta="visible" />
      <Property name="executionEnvironment" type="string"
        value="unspecified" meta="invisible" />
      <Property name="application" type="string" value="unspecified"
        meta="invisible" />
      <Property name="CPU" type="integer" value="" meta="invisible" />
      <Property name="RAM" type="integer" value="" meta="invisible" />
      <Property name="HD" type="integer" value="" meta="invisible" />
      <Property name="OS" type="string" value="" meta="invisible" />
      <Property name="Constraint" type="OCL" value="" meta="invisible" />
    </Properties>
    <Ports>
      <Port name="defaultPort" description="Default Port"
        id="server4_port1">
        <Properties>
          <Property name="Constraint" type="OCL" value="" meta="" />
        </Properties>
      </Port>
    </Ports>
  </Component>
  <Component name="StockServerInternational" type="server"
    description="external StockServer for international Lan" id="server5">
    <Properties>
      <Property name="physicalComponent" type="string"
        value="ExternalSystem" meta="visible" />
      <Property name="executionEnvironment" type="string"
        value="unspecified" meta="invisible" />
      <Property name="application" type="string" value="unspecified"
        meta="invisible" />
      <Property name="CPU" type="integer" value="" meta="invisible" />
      <Property name="RAM" type="integer" value="" meta="invisible" />
      <Property name="HD" type="integer" value="" meta="invisible" />
      <Property name="OS" type="string" value="" meta="invisible" />
      <Property name="Constraint" type="OCL" value="" meta="invisible" />
    </Properties>
    <Ports>
      <Port name="defaultPort" description="Default Port"
        id="server5_port1">
        <Properties>
          <Property name="Constraint" type="OCL" value="" meta="" />
        </Properties>
```

```
    </Port>
  </Ports>
</Component>
<Component name="PrintServer" type="server" description="external
  PrintServer for international Lan" id="server6">
  <Properties>
    <Property name="physicalComponent" type="string"
      value="ExternalSystem" meta="visible" />
    <Property name="executionEnvironment" type="string"
      value="unspecified" meta="invisible" />
    <Property name="application" type="string" value="unspecified"
      meta="invisible" />
    <Property name="CPU" type="integer" value="" meta="invisible" />
    <Property name="RAM" type="integer" value="" meta="invisible" />
    <Property name="HD" type="integer" value="" meta="invisible" />
    <Property name="OS" type="string" value="" meta="invisible" />
    <Property name="Constraint" type="OCL" value="" meta="invisible" />
  </Properties>
  <Ports>
    <Port name="defaultPort" description="Default Port"
      id="server6_port1">
      <Properties>
        <Property name="Constraint" type="OCL" value="" meta="" />
      </Properties>
    </Port>
  </Ports>
</Component>
<Component name="AccountinServer" type="server" description="external
  AccountingServer for international Lan" id="server7">
  <Properties>
    <Property name="physicalComponent" type="string"
      value="ExternalSystem" meta="visible" />
    <Property name="executionEnvironment" type="string"
      value="unspecified" meta="invisible" />
    <Property name="application" type="string" value="unspecified"
      meta="invisible" />
    <Property name="CPU" type="integer" value="" meta="invisible" />
    <Property name="RAM" type="integer" value="" meta="invisible" />
    <Property name="HD" type="integer" value="" meta="invisible" />
    <Property name="OS" type="string" value="" meta="invisible" />
    <Property name="Constraint" type="OCL" value="" meta="invisible" />
  </Properties>
  <Ports>
    <Port name="defaultPort" description="Default Port"
      id="server7_port1">
      <Properties>
        <Property name="Constraint" type="OCL" value="" meta="" />
      </Properties>
    </Port>
  </Ports>
</Component>
<Component name="ApplicationServerNational" type="server"
  description="ApplicationServer for national Lan" id="server8">
  <Properties>
    <Property name="physicalComponent" type="string" value="OfficeServer"
      meta="visible" />
    <Property name="executionEnvironment" type="string"
      value="ApplicationServer" meta="visible" />
    <Property name="application" type="string" value="unspecified"
      meta="invisible" />
    <Property name="CPU" type="Integer" value="2000" meta="visible" />
    <Property name="RAM" type="Integer" value="16384" meta="visible" />
    <Property name="HD" type="Integer" value="100" meta="visible" />
    <Property name="OS" type="String" value="SUSE" meta="visible" />
    <Property name="Constraint" type="OCL" value="" meta="invisible" />
  </Properties>
  <Ports>
    <Port name="defaultPort" description="Default Port"
```

```
        id="server8_port1">
        <Properties>
          <Property name="Constraint" type="OCL" value="" meta="" />
        </Properties>
      </Port>
    </Ports>
  </Component>
  <Component name="ApplicationServerInternational" type="server"
    description="ApplicationServer for international Lan" id="server9">
    <Properties>
      <Property name="physicalComponent" type="string" value="OfficeServer"
        meta="visible" />
      <Property name="executionEnvironment" type="string"
        value="ApplicationServer" meta="visible" />
      <Property name="application" type="string" value="unspecified"
        meta="invisible" />
      <Property name="CPU" type="Integer" value="2000" meta="visible" />
      <Property name="RAM" type="Integer" value="16384" meta="visible" />
      <Property name="HD" type="Integer" value="100" meta="visible" />
      <Property name="OS" type="String" value="SUSE" meta="visible" />
      <Property name="Constraint" type="OCL" value="" meta="invisible" />
    </Properties>
    <Ports>
      <Port name="defaultPort" description="Default Port"
        id="server9_port1">
        <Properties>
          <Property name="Constraint" type="OCL" value="" meta="" />
        </Properties>
      </Port>
    </Ports>
  </Component>
  <Component name="WebServer" type="server" description="WebServers"
    id="server10">
    <Properties>
      <Property name="physicalComponent" type="string" value="MainFrame"
        meta="visible" />
      <Property name="executionEnvironment" type="string"
        value="GenericContainer" meta="visible" />
      <Property name="application" type="string" value="WebServer"
        meta="visible" />
      <Property name="CPU" type="Integer" value="2000" meta="visible" />
      <Property name="RAM" type="Integer" value="16384" meta="visible" />
      <Property name="HD" type="Integer" value="100" meta="visible" />
      <Property name="OS" type="String" value="SUSE" meta="visible" />
      <Property name="Constraint" type="OCL" value="" meta="invisible" />
    </Properties>
    <Ports>
      <Port name="defaultPort" description="Default Port"
        id="server10_port1">
        <Properties>
          <Property name="Constraint" type="OCL" value="" meta="" />
        </Properties>
      </Port>
    </Ports>
  </Component>
</Components>
<Connectors>
  <Connector name="Internet" type="internet"
    description="Internetconnection" id="con1">
    <Properties>
      <Property name="Constraint" type="OCL" value="" meta="invisible" />
      <Property name="TransportProtocol" type="String" value="TCP/IP"
        meta="visible" />
      <Property name="Max_Bandwidth_mb" type="Integer" value="1000"
        meta="visible" />
    </Properties>
    <Roles>
      <Role name="customerPCRole" description="" port_ref="client1_port1"
```

```
      id="con1_role1">
      <Properties>
        <Property name="Constraint" type="OCL" value="" meta="" />
      </Properties>
    </Role>
    <Role name="customerMobileRole" description=""
      port_ref="client2_port1" id="con1_role2">
      <Properties>
        <Property name="Constraint" type="OCL" value="" meta="" />
      </Properties>
    </Role>
    <Role name="firewallNational" description=""
      port_ref="firewall1_port1" id="con1_role3">
      <Properties>
        <Property name="Constraint" type="OCL" value="" meta="" />
      </Properties>
    </Role>
    <Role name="firewallInternational" description=""
      port_ref="firewall2_port1" id="con1_role4">
      <Properties>
        <Property name="Constraint" type="OCL" value="" meta="" />
      </Properties>
    </Role>
    <Role name="firewallLoad" description="" port_ref="firewall3_port1"
      id="con1_role5">
      <Properties>
        <Property name="Constraint" type="OCL" value="" meta="" />
      </Properties>
    </Role>
    <Role name="billing" description="" port_ref="server1_port1"
      id="con1_role6">
      <Properties>
        <Property name="Constraint" type="OCL" value="" meta="" />
      </Properties>
    </Role>
    <Role name="supplier" description="" port_ref="server2_port1"
      id="con1_role7">
      <Properties>
        <Property name="Constraint" type="OCL" value="" meta="" />
      </Properties>
    </Role>
    <Role name="content" description="" port_ref="server3_port1"
      id="con1_role8">
      <Properties>
        <Property name="Constraint" type="OCL" value="" meta="" />
      </Properties>
    </Role>
  </Roles>
</Connector>
<Connector name="NationalLan" type="lan" description="national Lan"
  id="con2">
  <Properties>
    <Property name="Constraint" type="OCL" value="" meta="invisible" />
    <Property name="TransportProtocol" type="String" value="TCP/IP"
      meta="visible" />
    <Property name="Max_Bandwidth_mb" type="Integer" value="2048"
      meta="visible" />
  </Properties>
  <Roles>
    <Role name="adminRole" description="" port_ref="client3_port1"
      id="con2_role1">
      <Properties>
        <Property name="Constraint" type="OCL" value="" meta="" />
      </Properties>
    </Role>
    <Role name="subscriber" description="" port_ref="subscriber1_port1"
      id="con2_role3">
      <Properties>
```

```
      <Property name="Constraint" type="OCL" value="" meta="" />
    </Properties>
  </Role>
  <Role name="stock" description="" port_ref="server4_port1"
    id="con2_role4">
    <Properties>
      <Property name="Constraint" type="OCL" value="" meta="" />
    </Properties>
  </Role>
  <Role name="print" description="" port_ref="server6_port1"
    id="con2_role5">
    <Properties>
      <Property name="Constraint" type="OCL" value="" meta="" />
    </Properties>
  </Role>
  <Role name="appserver" description="" port_ref="server8_port1"
    id="con2_role2">
    <Properties>
      <Property name="Constraint" type="OCL" value="" meta="" />
    </Properties>
  </Role>
 </Roles>
</Connector>
<Connector name="InternationalLan" type="lan" description="International
      Lan" id="con3">
  <Properties>
    <Property name="Constraint" type="OCL" value="" meta="invisible" />
    <Property name="TransportProtocol" type="String" value="TCP/IP"
      meta="visible" />
    <Property name="Max_Bandwidth_mb" type="Integer" value="2048"
      meta="visible" />
  </Properties>
  <Roles>
    <Role name="firewall" description="" port_ref="firewall4_port1"
      id="con3_role1">
      <Properties>
        <Property name="Constraint" type="OCL" value="" meta="" />
      </Properties>
    </Role>
    <Role name="database" description="" port_ref="database1_port1"
      id="con3_role2">
      <Properties>
        <Property name="Constraint" type="OCL" value="" meta="" />
      </Properties>
    </Role>
    <Role name="admin" description="" port_ref="client4_port1"
      id="con3_role3">
      <Properties>
        <Property name="Constraint" type="OCL" value="" meta="" />
      </Properties>
    </Role>
    <Role name="publisher" description="" port_ref="publisher1_port1"
      id="con3_role4">
      <Properties>
        <Property name="Constraint" type="OCL" value="" meta="" />
      </Properties>
    </Role>
    <Role name="appserver" description="" port_ref="server9_port1"
      id="con3_role5">
      <Properties>
        <Property name="Constraint" type="OCL" value="" meta="" />
      </Properties>
    </Role>
    <Role name="accounting" description="" port_ref="server7_port1"
      id="con3_role6">
      <Properties>
        <Property name="Constraint" type="OCL" value="" meta="" />
      </Properties>
```

```
      </Role>
      <Role name="stock" description="" port_ref="server5_port1"
        id="con3_role7">
        <Properties>
          <Property name="Constraint" type="OCL" value="" meta="" />
        </Properties>
      </Role>
    </Roles>
  </Connector>
  <Connector name="Web2Load" type="intranet" description="Intranet between
    webserver and loadbalancer" id="con5">
    <Properties>
      <Property name="Constraint" type="OCL" value="" meta="invisible" />
      <Property name="TransportProtocol" type="String" value="TCP/IP"
        meta="visible" />
      <Property name="Max_Bandwidth_mb" type="Integer" value="2048"
        meta="visible" />
    </Properties>
    <Roles>
      <Role name="web" description="" port_ref="server10_port1"
        id="con5_role1">
        <Properties>
          <Property name="Constraint" type="OCL" value="" meta="" />
        </Properties>
      </Role>
      <Role name="load" description="" port_ref="loadbalancer1_port1"
        id="con5_role2">
        <Properties>
          <Property name="Constraint" type="OCL" value="" meta="" />
        </Properties>
      </Role>
    </Roles>
  </Connector>
  <Connector name="Load2Firewall" type="intranet" description="Intranet
    between Loadbalancer and firewall" id="con6">
    <Properties>
      <Property name="Constraint" type="OCL" value="" meta="invisible" />
      <Property name="TransportProtocol" type="String" value="TCP/IP"
        meta="visible" />
      <Property name="Max_Bandwidth_mb" type="Integer" value="2048"
        meta="visible" />
    </Properties>
    <Roles>
      <Role name="fire" description="" port_ref="firewall3_port1"
        id="con6_role1">
        <Properties>
          <Property name="Constraint" type="OCL" value="" meta="" />
        </Properties>
      </Role>
      <Role name="load" description="" port_ref="loadbalancer1_port1"
        id="con6_role2">
        <Properties>
          <Property name="Constraint" type="OCL" value="" meta="" />
        </Properties>
      </Role>
    </Roles>
  </Connector>
  <Connector name="Fire2Web" type="intranet"
    description="Firewall2WebServer" id="con7">
    <Properties>
      <Property name="Constraint" type="OCL" value="" meta="invisible" />
      <Property name="TransportProtocol" type="String" value="TCP/IP"
        meta="visible" />
      <Property name="Max_Bandwidth_mb" type="Integer" value="2048"
        meta="visible" />
    </Properties>
    <Roles>
      <Role name="fire" description="" port_ref="firewall4_port1"
```

```
          id="con7_role1">
          <Properties>
            <Property name="Constraint" type="OCL" value="" meta="" />
          </Properties>
        </Role>
        <Role name="web" description="" port_ref="server10_port1"
          id="con7_role2">
          <Properties>
            <Property name="Constraint" type="OCL" value="" meta="" />
          </Properties>
        </Role>
      </Roles>
    </Connector>
    <Connector name="NatApp2Fire" type="intranet" description="Connection
      between national AppServer &amp; Firewall" id="con8">
      <Properties>
        <Property name="Constraint" type="OCL" value="" meta="invisible" />
        <Property name="TransportProtocol" type="String" value="TCP/IP"
          meta="visible" />
        <Property name="Max_Bandwidth_mb" type="Integer" value="2048"
          meta="visible" />
      </Properties>
      <Roles>
        <Role name="fire" description="" port_ref="firewall1_port1"
          id="con8_role1">
          <Properties>
            <Property name="Constraint" type="OCL" value="" meta="" />
          </Properties>
        </Role>
        <Role name="appserver" description="" port_ref="server8_port1"
          id="con8_role2">
          <Properties>
            <Property name="Constraint" type="OCL" value="" meta="" />
          </Properties>
        </Role>
      </Roles>
    </Connector>
    <Connector name="IntApp2Fire" type="intranet" description="Connection
      between international AppServer &amp; Firewall" id="con4">
      <Properties>
        <Property name="Constraint" type="OCL" value="" meta="invisible" />
        <Property name="TransportProtocol" type="String" value="TCP/IP"
          meta="visible" />
        <Property name="Max_Bandwidth_mb" type="Integer" value="2048"
          meta="visible" />
      </Properties>
      <Roles>
        <Role name="firewall" description="" port_ref="firewall2_port1"
          id="con4_role1">
          <Properties>
            <Property name="Constraint" type="OCL" value="" meta="" />
          </Properties>
        </Role>
        <Role name="appserver" description="" port_ref="server9_port1"
          id="con4_role2">
          <Properties>
            <Property name="Constraint" type="OCL" value="" meta="" />
          </Properties>
        </Role>
      </Roles>
    </Connector>
  </Connectors>
  <Compositions />
  <TransponderIDs />
</Project>
```

Because the original intention was to let another company deal with the implementation of the software upon the built system the IT-officer needs to export the project to some kind of further usable format.

The decision falls to the ctb-format because the company already found a consignee which uses the Component Toolbox for creating software architectures. So he executes the exportation function of the HSAM-Tool which generates the following ctb-file:

```
<?xml version="1.0" encoding="UTF 8"?>
<ctb:Diagram xmi:version="2.0" xmlns:xmi="http://www.omg.org/XMI"
  xmlns:xsi="http://www.w3.org/2001/XMLSchema-instance"
  xmlns:ctb="http://ctb.com">
  <physicalComponents xsi:type="ctb:PhysicalComponent" Typ="WorkStation">
    <executionEnvironments Typ="GenericContainer" />
  </physicalComponents>
  <physicalComponents xsi:type="ctb:PhysicalComponent" Typ="MobileDevice">
    <executionEnvironments Typ="MidletContainer" />
  </physicalComponents>
  <physicalComponents xsi:type="ctb:PhysicalComponent" Typ="WorkStation"
    CPU="2400" RAM="2048" HD="80" OS="WinXP">
    <executionEnvironments Typ="GenericContainer" />
  </physicalComponents>
  <physicalComponents xsi:type="ctb:PhysicalComponent" Typ="WorkStation"
    CPU="2400" RAM="2048" HD="80" OS="WinXP">
    <executionEnvironments Typ="GenericContainer" />
  </physicalComponents>
  <physicalComponents xsi:type="ctb:PhysicalComponent" Typ="GenericDevice">
    <executionEnvironments Typ="GenericContainer">
      <applications Typ="Firewall" />
    </executionEnvironments>
  </physicalComponents>
  <physicalComponents xsi:type="ctb:PhysicalComponent" Typ="GenericDevice">
    <executionEnvironments Typ="GenericContainer">
      <applications Typ="Firewall" />
    </executionEnvironments>
  </physicalComponents>
  <physicalComponents xsi:type="ctb:PhysicalComponent" Typ="GenericDevice">
    <executionEnvironments Typ="GenericContainer">
      <applications Typ="Firewall" />
    </executionEnvironments>
  </physicalComponents>
  <physicalComponents xsi:type="ctb:PhysicalComponent" Typ="GenericDevice">
    <executionEnvironments Typ="GenericContainer">
      <applications Typ="Firewall" />
    </executionEnvironments>
  </physicalComponents>
  <physicalComponents xsi:type="ctb:PhysicalComponent" Typ="GenericDevice">
    <executionEnvironments Typ="GenericContainer">
      <applications Typ="LoadBalancer" />
    </executionEnvironments>
  </physicalComponents>
  <physicalComponents xsi:type="ctb:PhysicalComponent" Typ="MainFrame"
    CPU="3000" RAM="8192" HD="160" OS="SUSE">
    <executionEnvironments Typ="GenericContainer">
      <applications Typ="Database" />
    </executionEnvironments>
  </physicalComponents>
  <physicalComponents xsi:type="ctb:PhysicalComponent" Typ="MainFrame"
    CPU="2400" RAM="8192" HD="160" OS="SUSE">
    <executionEnvironments Typ="GenericContainer">
      <applications Typ="MessagingSystem" />
    </executionEnvironments>
  </physicalComponents>
  <physicalComponents xsi:type="ctb:PhysicalComponent" Typ="MainFrame"
    CPU="2400" RAM="8192" HD="120" OS="SUSE">
    <executionEnvironments Typ="GenericContainer">
      <applications Typ="MessagingSystem" />
    </executionEnvironments>
```

```
</physicalComponents>
<externalSystems Functionality="BillingServer" />
<externalSystems Functionality="SupplierServer" />
<externalSystems Functionality="ContentServer" />
<externalSystems Functionality="StockServerNational" />
<externalSystems Functionality="StockServerInternational" />
<externalSystems Functionality="PrintServer" />
<externalSystems Functionality="AccountinServer" />
<physicalComponents xsi:type="ctb:PhysicalComponent" Typ="OfficeServer"
  CPU="2000" RAM="16384" HD="100" OS="SUSE">
  <executionEnvironments Typ="ApplicationServer" />
</physicalComponents>
<physicalComponents xsi:type="ctb:PhysicalComponent" Typ="OfficeServer"
  CPU="2000" RAM="16384" HD="100" OS="SUSE">
  <executionEnvironments Typ="ApplicationServer" />
</physicalComponents>
<physicalComponents xsi:type="ctb:PhysicalComponent" Typ="MainFrame"
  CPU="2000" RAM="16384" HD="100" OS="SUSE">
  <executionEnvironments Typ="GenericContainer">
    <applications Typ="WebServer" />
  </executionEnvironments>
</physicalComponents>
<networks NetworkTyp="internet" TransportProtocol="TCP/IP"
  Max_Bandwidth_mb="1000" />
<networks NetworkTyp="lan" TransportProtocol="TCP/IP"
  Max_Bandwidth_mb="2048" />
<networks NetworkTyp="lan" TransportProtocol="TCP/IP"
  Max_Bandwidth_mb="2048" />
<networks NetworkTyp="intranet" TransportProtocol="TCP/IP"
  Max_Bandwidth_mb="2048" />
<networks NetworkTyp="intranet" TransportProtocol="TCP/IP"
  Max_Bandwidth_mb="2048" />
<networks NetworkTyp="intranet" TransportProtocol="TCP/IP"
  Max_Bandwidth_mb="2048" />
<networks NetworkTyp="intranet" TransportProtocol="TCP/IP"
  Max_Bandwidth_mb="2048" />
<networks NetworkTyp="intranet" TransportProtocol="TCP/IP"
  Max_Bandwidth_mb="2048" />
<networkConnections targetNetwork="//@networks.0"
  sourceComponent="//@physicalComponents.0" />
<networkConnections targetNetwork="//@networks.0"
  sourceComponent="//@physicalComponents.1" />
<networkConnections targetNetwork="//@networks.0"
  sourceComponent="//@physicalComponents.4" />
<networkConnections targetNetwork="//@networks.0"
  sourceComponent="//@physicalComponents.5" />
<networkConnections targetNetwork="//@networks.0"
  sourceComponent="//@physicalComponents.6" />
<networkConnections targetNetwork="//@networks.0"
  sourceComponent="//@externalSystems.0" />
<networkConnections targetNetwork="//@networks.0"
  sourceComponent="//@externalSystems.1" />
<networkConnections targetNetwork="//@networks.0"
  sourceComponent="//@externalSystems.2" />
<networkConnections targetNetwork="//@networks.1"
  sourceComponent="//@physicalComponents.2" />
<networkConnections targetNetwork="//@networks.1"
  sourceComponent="//@physicalComponents.11" />
<networkConnections targetNetwork="//@networks.1"
  sourceComponent="//@externalSystems.3" />
<networkConnections targetNetwork="//@networks.1"
  sourceComponent="//@externalSystems.5" />
<networkConnections targetNetwork="//@networks.1"
  sourceComponent="//@physicalComponents.12" />
<networkConnections targetNetwork="//@networks.2"
  sourceComponent="//@physicalComponents.7" />
<networkConnections targetNetwork="//@networks.2"
  sourceComponent="//@physicalComponents.9" />
```

```
  <networkConnections targetNetwork="//@networks.2"
    sourceComponent="//@physicalComponents.3" />
  <networkConnections targetNetwork="//@networks.2"
    sourceComponent="//@physicalComponents.10" />
  <networkConnections targetNetwork="//@networks.2"
    sourceComponent="//@physicalComponents.13" />
  <networkConnections targetNetwork="//@networks.2"
    sourceComponent="//@externalSystems.6" />
  <networkConnections targetNetwork="//@networks.2"
    sourceComponent="//@externalSystems.4" />
  <networkConnections targetNetwork="//@networks.3"
    sourceComponent="//@physicalComponents.14" />
  <networkConnections targetNetwork="//@networks.3"
    sourceComponent="//@physicalComponents.8" />
  <networkConnections targetNetwork="//@networks.4"
    sourceComponent="//@physicalComponents.6" />
  <networkConnections targetNetwork="//@networks.4"
    sourceComponent="//@physicalComponents.8" />
  <networkConnections targetNetwork="//@networks.5"
    sourceComponent="//@physicalComponents.7" />
  <networkConnections targetNetwork="//@networks.5"
    sourceComponent="//@physicalComponents.14" />
  <networkConnections targetNetwork="//@networks.6"
    sourceComponent="//@physicalComponents.4" />
  <networkConnections targetNetwork="//@networks.6"
    sourceComponent="//@physicalComponents.12" />
  <networkConnections targetNetwork="//@networks.7"
    sourceComponent="//@physicalComponents.5" />
  <networkConnections targetNetwork="//@networks.7"
    sourceComponent="//@physicalComponents.13" />
</ctb:Diagram>
```


This file is now the interface to be provided for the consignee who is willing to implement the software architecture upon the company's system. Together with the functional description of the web shop the IT-officer hands this exportation over to the implementing company and with that finishes the process of HSAM.

Chapter 7
Conclusion

This book introduced a new haptic approach to create system architectures. It can be used to develop, build, communicate, and file such architectures.

In the beginning, there was a discussion about the state of the art. Today, software and system architects need to fulfill widespread requirements which start at being a technical advisor and end as communicator of the architecture to all kinds of stakeholders. As systems and software become more complex these days, the role of the architects becomes more and more important. Still there is no defined standard for them to use. Most of the instruments, they have access to, are highly sophisticated and specialized for a specific intention.

The new approach shows a haptic and very intuitive way for how system architecture can be created, documented, configured, communicated, and filed. The idea is to build an architecture with the help of Lego. Each element in a system is represented by a composition of Lego bricks which are listed in a catalogue. The working team can create the system's architecture by combining every single representation to one big building. In order to guarantee further proceeding of the resulting architecture, a tool is presented. With the help of this tool the architects have the possibility to read in the building using RFID-technology, to configure the architecture using the provided functionalities, and to export the system to ACME or CTB.

This new kind of approach to create a system's architecture has a lot of advantages over the existing ones. At the first place, there is its intuitive way of the actual building process. Everybody has an idea of how to handle Lego bricks. There are no real constraints for building the system. The next thing is that this approach invites the architects to work at the same time at the same project. So it highly supports teamwork and consequently the feedback and communication between the architects during the actual working process. Because of its intuitive way and the fact that one can overlook the whole architecture with one glance, the approach is very suited to support the communication of the underlying system to stakeholders, who do not have the background to understand a system's architecture

A. Weber and S. Dustdar, *Haptic Systems Architecture Modeling*,
DOI 10.1007/978-3-7091-0755-3_7, © Springer-Verlag/Wien 2012

all by themselves. Moreover, with the Component Toolbox there is a tool which supports the exporting file format ctb. With the help of Component Toolbox the architects have the possibility to build a software architecture on top of the system which exactly fits the underlying architecture. Because of the flexibility of Lego bricks and the fact that the HSAM-Tool is based on XML-files the whole approach is very extensible and thus adaptable.

Further studies could include the exact definition for additional system architectural elements. Consequently a representation in Lego needs to be found for those new elements. Validation of existing element Lego representations as well as of the new ones is also required through testing the compositions in more practical case studies. Default properties for each element are also subject to further research.

For the HSAM-Tool the process of user interaction should be analyzed and improved and the whole program of course could be revised and adapted for special needs. Currently the program is set to handle the presented case study with no problems. There might be minor programming issues for additional projects which need to be taken care of to guarantee a smooth operation.

Addendum

Installation

Prerequisites are:

- Microsoft .NET Framework 3.0
  [https://www.microsoft.com/downloads/details.aspx?FamilyID = 10cc340b-f857-4a14-83f5-25634c3bf043&DisplayLang = en]
- Driver for RFID-Reader
  [http://acg-id.aaitg.com/index.php?id = 156]
- Optional:
  To run the Microsoft Visual C# 2005 project the Microsoft Visual C# Express Edition 2005 is required
  [http://msdn2.microsoft.com/en-us/express/aa700756.aspx]

  You can download the HSAM-Tool and its documentation at:
  www.infosys.tuwien.ac.at/HSAM-Book

A. Weber and S. Dustdar, *Haptic Systems Architecture Modeling*,
DOI 10.1007/978-3-7091-0755-3, © Springer-Verlag/Wien 2012

Bibliography

ABLE – architecture based languages and environments (2007) Retrieved July 4, 2007, from The Acme ADL: http://www.cs.cmu.edu/~acme/

ACG ID (n.d.) (2007) ACG ID. Retrieved October 4, 2007, from http://acg-id.aaitg.com/index.php

Bass L, Clements P, Kazman R (1998) Software architecture in practice. Addison Wesley Longman, USA

Bhuptani M, Moradpour S (2005) RFID field guide – deploying radio frequency identification systems. Prentice Hall Professional Technical Reference, Upper Saddle River

Birkhölzer T, Vaupel J (2003) IT-architekturen: planung, integration, wartung. VDE Verlag GMBH, Berlin

Bray T, Paoli J, Sperberg C, Maler E, Yergeau F (2006) Extensible markup language (XML) 1.0 (4th edn.). (W3C) Retrieved Jänner 23, 2007, from http://www.w3.org/TR/2006/REC-xml-20060816/

Broy M, Spaniol O (1999) VDI-Lexikon Informatik und Kommunikationstechnik. Springer, Berlin

Dustdar S, Gall H, Hauswirth M (2003) Software-Architekturen für verteilte Systeme. Springer Verlag, Berlin

Fielding R, Gettys J, Mogul J, Frystyk H, Masinter L, Leach P et al (1999) Hypertext transport protocol – HTTP/1.1. *RFC2616*

Finkenzeller K (2002) RFID-Handbuch. Carl Hanser Verlag, München

Gudgin M, Hadley M, Mendelsohn N, Moreau J-J, Frystyk Nielsen H (2003) SOAP Version 1.2 Part 1: Messaging framework. (W3C) Retrieved Jänner 23, 2007, from http://www.w3.org/TR/2003/REC-soap12-part1-20030624/

Hofstetter U (2007) Component toolbox – a toolbox for architectural design. University of Zurich, Software Evolution and Architecture Lab, Zürich

Information Science Institute, University of Southern California (1981) Transmission control protocol. *RFC793*

Klensin J (2001) Simple mail transfer protocol. *RFC2821*

Klußmann N (2000) Lexikon der Kommunikations- und Informationstechnik. Hüthig, Heidelberg

LEGO Group (2007) The official website of lego. Retrieved September 28, 2007, from http://www.lego.com/en-US/default.aspx

Lévy N, Losavio F, Matteo A (1998) Comparing architectural styles: broker specializes mediatior. ACM, Newyork

Naumovich G (2002) Using the observer design pattern for implementation of data flow analyses. ACM, Newyork

NXP (2007) NXP semiconductors. Retrieved September 29, 2007, from MIFARE Classic: http://www.nxp.com/acrobat_download/other/identification/m001052.pdf

A. Weber and S. Dustdar, *Haptic Systems Architecture Modeling*,
DOI 10.1007/978-3-7091-0755-3, © Springer-Verlag/Wien 2012

OMG – Object Management Group (n.d.) (2007) Unified modeling language. Retrieved July 3, 2007, from http://www.omg.org/technology/documents/formal/uml.htm

Postel J (1980) User datagram protocol. *RFC768*

Postel J, Reynolds J (1985) File transfer protocol (FTP). *RFC959*

Shaw M, David G (1996) Software architecture – perspectives on an emerging discipline. Simon & Schuster, Upper Saddle River

Sun Developer Network (n.d.) (2007) Sun developer network (SDN). Retrieved Jänner 23, 2007, from Java Database Connectivity (JDBC): http://java.sun.com/javase/technologies/database/index.jsp

TAGnology RFID Ltd (2006) RFIDwebshop. Retrieved September 19, 2007, from http://www.rfid-webshop.com/shop/product_info.php/info/p603_TAGmobi-USB—MIFARE.html

TAGnology RFID Ltd (2006) RFIDwebshop. Retrieved September 19, 2007, from http://www.rfid-webshop.com/shop/product_info.php/info/p488_Smart-Control-Label-25x9mm–MIFARE-1k–self-adhesive.html

Tate J, Lucchese F, Moore R (2006) Introduction to storage area networks. ibm.com/redbooks

Vogel O, Arnold I, Chughtai A, Ihler E, Mehlig U, Neumann T et al (2005) Software-Architektur: Grundlagen – Konzepte – Praxis. Elsevier Gmbh, München

Wikipedia (2007) Wikipedia, the free encyclopedia. Retrieved September 14., 2007, from http://en.wikipedia.org/wiki/Load_balancing_%28computing%29

Zdun U, Avgeriou P (2005) Modelling architectural patterns using architectural primitives. ACM, Newyork

Printing: Ten Brink, Meppel, The Netherlands
Binding: Stürtz, Würzburg, Germany